The Partner Hacker Handbook

ANTHOLOGY ON ECOSYSTEMS
Volume 1

PARTNER HACKER

PARTNER HACKER

Table of Contents

Foreword

Jay McBain is the Chief Analyst at Canalys. He is an accomplished speaker, author, and innovator in the IT industry.

He was named 2022 Channel Influencer of the Year by Channel Partners Magazine, Top 40 Under Forty by the Business Review, Channel A-List by CRN, Top 8 Thought Leader by Channel Marketing Journal, Top 20 Visionary by ChannelPro, Top 25 Newsmaker by CDN Magazine, Top 50 Channel Influencer by Penton, Top 100 Most Respected Thought Leader by VSR Magazine, Global Power 150 by SMB Magazine, and Top 250 Managed Services Executives by MSPmentor.

by Jay McBain

We're at the beginning of a once-in-a-generation shift in the global economy.

Going it alone is not an option.

Tech companies across the spectrum are rethinking their approach to distribution, adjusting to the new realities of customer buying habits and an expanding software stack that must interoperate.

I've called it the Decade of the Ecosystem.

A shift this big needs a voice. There are dozens of watering holes in the enterprise and tech channel world. I've been following most of them for much of my career.

But the transformation from the traditional channel to the ecosystem requires new ideas, new frameworks, and a new lexicon.

I've developed a bit of a reputation for communicating with lots of data. I can give you stats to validate every trend and inform every prediction. But humans will lead the decade of the ecosystem and humans need more than data. Humans need narratives. They need stories and mental models that connect the dots of data into an understandable arc.

When PartnerHacker emerged on the scene in early 2022, I spotted a new storyteller for this era. They provided a voice to this nascent movement, a rallying flag for all those laboring in the fields of partnerships and ecosystems.

There is a lot of work to be done—particularly in bringing together the emergent class of partner-focused startups with the established enterprise teams and the world of traditional channel. That work begins with ideas and conversations. It ends in a total transformation of business as we know it.

This handbook is a small step forward in the conversation. I have a feeling it will only get better with age, as the ideas and predictions in these pages are proven in the world.

We're still early. Which means those who see the shift, participate in the conversation, and adjust their lives and business strategies accordingly have a first mover advantage.

I'm excited to be a part of the next phase in this decade-defining shift, and I'm thrilled to see PartnerHacker and all the contributors to this volume join me on the adventure.

Are you ready?

The PartnerHacker Manifesto: Trust is the New Data

By Jared Fuller

Jared Fuller is the co-founder of PartnerHacker and co-host of the PartnerUp podcast.

Article originally published on the PartnerHacker website.

Announcing the launch of PartnerHacker.com and the global shift that led to it.

Let's Go Back

It seems like just yesterday. 2006. My graduation year. The year British mathematician and marketing executive Clive Humby boldly proclaimed,

"Data is the new oil."

We were at the beginning of a massive change. Cell phones went from luxury to ubiquitous. SMS became our primary method of communication with friends and family.

The world's information was now at our fingertips and in our pockets.

Myspace ruled the social zeitgeist where relationships and communities were built. Everyone was a creator. I was recording and "mastering" tracks from my band Prophecy for the Damned. (Ask me about that over drinks sometime.)

For the first time, the experience of sharing and discovering online became normal not only for me, but for all of us. Clive Humby was right. After his prophecy, the race for digital value was on. Mass quantities of data were mined, centralized, and monetized.

Not just by private companies, but also governments. Remember the Patriot Act? The NSA? Wikileaks and Edward Snowden? **Everyone** wanted the digits.

And the winners reaped mass rewards. Both B2C and B2B businesses alike. Amazon shares traded at around $30 in 2006. In 2022, they traded around $3,000. A 10,000% increase in value. Salesforce shares traded at $6 in 2006. In 2022, $300. A 5,000% increase in value.

For B2C and B2B, data really was the new oil.

That is, until data polluted the world. What was once signal became noise. What was once convenient became inconvenient.

Data was the new oil. Until data lost our trust.

Now, **trust is the new data.**

The Changing B2B World

Before the Digital World was normal, we lived in the Brand World.

In the Brand World, B2B companies primarily relied on indirect channels. For example, telecom companies dominated the business landscape like SaaS companies do today.

For them, "going to market" required a deep understanding and partnership with the indirect players. Back then, B2B companies could hardly measure the ROI of direct marketing. Furthermore, access to their buyers was full of gatekeepers. Therefore, partners played an essential role in acquiring, selling, and servicing customers.

For many of us who have lived in the B2B SaaS world for the past decade or two, "indirect" hasn't been our normal. Simply put, indirect channels weren't needed during the shift to the software-eaten, data-driven world the same way they were in the past. B2B companies could acquire new customers cheaply and efficiently. Data amassed by Google, Facebook, and others allowed companies direct access to new customers with high margins and low acquisition costs.

Platforms like Salesforce precipitated the centralization of customer data and begat entirely new categories of sales digitization and marketing automation, further accelerating the arms race for digital oil.

The origins of "indirect," "channel," or "business development," as it was taught for other industries, wasn't the world that SaaS natives grew up in. SaaS companies, instead, could control their own destiny, it seemed, without reliance or partnership with third parties.

After 20 years of SaaS models, less than 30% of SaaS sales are indirect, and most of those are through a small number of global enterprises like Microsoft.

Sirius Decisions predicts indirect sales will continue to shrink every year for the next decade. And yet... Salesforce claims they will recruit 250,000 new partners over the next four years while at the same time effectively shutting down their reseller program. And yet... even with all of the centralization and exploitation of data, according to the WTO, 75% of trade is still indirect.

Wait, what? What gives? Something must be changing. Again.

The Eras

B2B SaaS companies with enduring aspirations must recognize that what got them here will not get them there.

At PartnerHacker, we believe we are in the midst of a "Partnerships Moment" that will mark a new cycle for business.

A new era.

The Three Eras of B2B provide a lens to look back in order to look forward.

- The Era of Sales Digitization (2000's)
- The Era of Marketing Automation (2010's)
- The Era of Partner Ecosystems (2020 +)

The first two eras were underpinned by one dominant concept. Data.

The "cloud" democratized access to read, update, and analyze data at scales previously unthinkable. Entire industries were born and others entirely disrupted. For the first time ever in sales, everything could be tracked to the decimal. And then, for the first time ever in marketing, everything could be automated.

For the past decade, we've been living in this era of marketing automation. A time defined by technology and direct access to a new market of customers. When one growth channel stopped producing ROI, new channels seemed to emerge to fill the void.

Methods and access to market were innovating so rapidly that legacy indirect channels failed to adapt at the same pace. New technologies empowered a new generation of companies and jobs where they could build, market, sell, deploy, and retain directly.

In the Era of Marketing Automation, digitally native B2B SaaS companies had little to no indirect business. Data was the fuel. Automation was the accelerant. Heck, large swaths of B2B companies even have it in their category names! "Digital Acceleration," "Sales Acceleration," "Revenue Acceleration."

But now, consumers are sick of the acceleration.

We've been polluted.

The Shift

There have been some exceptions. SaaS and Marketing Automation natives like Salesforce, and more recently HubSpot, leveraged and adopted indirect relationships and interdependence to grow their market presence and establish industry dominance.

But they did it differently.

As they grew, their partner models looked less like their predecessors (IT channel of old) and a transformation of traditional partner channel began.

Jay McBain (formerly of Forrester and now Chief Analyst at Canalys) summarized this transformation as the trifurcation of the channel, where partners began to affect different parts of the value chain.

He summarized the trifurcated channel as the Influencer Channel, Transactional Channel, and Retention Channel.

1. Influencer Channel

With buyers spending 68% of their journey digitally before speaking with a salesperson (direct or partner) and an astounding 71% of them reaching vendor selection after a digital-only journey, brands are wising up to the importance of getting in front of customers early and often. The "influencer channel" is made up of affinity partners, referrals, advocates, agencies, ambassadors, and alliances. Unlike channels of the past, these partners influence the buying process but are not involved in the transaction.

2. Transactional Channel

The traditional "transactional channel" doesn't go away. In fact, partners that have spent years on the "long-tail" list may actually find a home somewhere else in the program that has, up till now, only pushed them to resell. Tweaking channel data management, automation, insights, onboarding, incentives, co-selling, and co-marketing will determine winners and losers in this era.

3. Retention Channel

Knowing that the customer journey never ends in a subscription scenario and that brands need to re-earn a customer's business, partners that can drive adoption, ongoing customer experience, and the ability to upsell and cross-sell become critically important as the "retention channel." These partners appear as consultants, integrators, adjacent ISVs, digital agencies, etc.

Channel leaders of the past expected their partners to execute all three. Until they didn't.

Today, some partners affect one motion sometimes, and other partners affect others at other times. The lines have blurred. Jay's Forrester research predicted that they would blur further. And they did.

His prediction from a few years ago about millions of shadow channels entering the market came true. When looking through his trifurcated lens, more than 80% of (potential) partners are showing up before or after the sale, breaking the transactional mold.

Even Brand World natives with legacy channels like Microsoft, Adobe, Oracle, SAP, and Intuit are changing their indirect motions for this new era. As Jay pointed out, Microsoft, in 2019, "[A]nnounced that 7,500 new partners were joining their program each month. What it didn't announce is that 80% of those partners were non transacting."

In the Era of Partner Ecosystems, enduring B2B companies won't rely on traditional transacting indirect channels.

Goodbye phrases like "partner sourced" and "partner sold." And goodbye easy access to direct channels from cheap data.

In the Era of Partner Ecosystems, enduring B2B companies won't rely on data. In the Era of Partner Ecosystems, enduring B2B companies will rely on **trust.**

The winners will rely on partner ecosystems.

The Era of Partner Ecosystems

In the Era of Partner Ecosystems, enduring B2B SaaS companies create, nurture, and leverage their Ecosystem as core to their business. They value their Ecosystem the same way they value their customers, their products, and their team.

For these companies, Customer Experience and Partner Experience require the same standards. As the world exits the Era of Marketing Automation, it's time to codify what it means to live in this new world.

My former boss and founder of Drift, David Cancel, often claimed the leadership principles we aspired to were "simple, not easy." We experience his words first-hand and daily. He's right. But most first principles are much simpler to understand than they are to live by.

Yet the inverse feels more true for building partnerships and communities in the Era of Partner Ecosystems. "Complex, not difficult," might be how best to describe it. While building for or in ecosystems today isn't rocket science, there are dozens of incalculable elements.

Partners of all types need to be prioritized, found, recruited, onboarded, educated, trained, incentivized, motivated, loyal, and have the I.P. and tools necessary to promote, transact, or service a product.

It's complex but comprised of all things that great SaaS companies strive to be great at. Complex, but not difficult. The challenge is that our Ecosystem is not on payroll. The impact won't easily flow through financial models and spit out clean forecasts.

That's not to say we won't look to leading and lagging indicators of success or projections/analyses of investment, profit, and loss, but that the investments and contributions require a different lens and model to create and understand its impact. And new technologies to help.

The 2021 Channel Technology Landscape from Forrester showed a fast growing $5.7B market in channel technologies. Scott Brinker covered it in 2022 under the wider lens of partner technologies as the fastest growing technology sector in B2B, with 487% growth.

High performers are prioritizing partner ecosystem strategies.

In 2021, <u>IBM's Institute for Business Value surveyed over 3,000 CEOs</u> at high performing companies and found that building new ecosystems and partnerships was their top priority for enhancing customer experience and trust over the next two to three years (48%).

Underperformers, on the contrary, ranked it last (24%).

Dedication to partner and business ecosystems are changing the game for all. From executives, to managers, to individuals, all must incorporate how they contribute to and leverage ecosystems as a core part of their day, week, month, quarter, and year-in-the-life

What are Partner Ecosystems?

So what are partner, B2B, or business ecosystems anyway?

We can look to ecological systems to start. Natural ecosystems. Good ol' Mother Nature here on Earth. The simple definition:

- An Ecosystem (or ecological system) consists of all the organisms and the physical environment with which they interact. These biotic and abiotic components are linked together through nutrient cycles and energy flows.

And counterintuitively,

- Ecosystems with higher biodiversity tend to be more stable with greater resistance and resilience in the face of disturbances, or disruptive events.

And,

- In ecosystems, both matter and energy are conserved. Energy flows through the system—usually from light to heat— while matter is recycled.

Let's break down what this means for B2B ecosystems – and attempt to define B2B partner ecosystems fully:

A B2B Ecosystem consists of all networked accounts and contacts linked to the commerce and information they share.

B2B Ecosystems manifest in the form of Partners (accounts) and Communities (individuals) that either directly or indirectly benefit the end Customer (user) of the B2B Ecosystem parent.

Partners are companies with a shared commercial interest. Communities are individuals with a shared professional interest.

The environments in which they interact are defined by markets and often (but not always) segmented by vertical (industry), horizontal (persona), segment (size), and territory (geography).

These components are linked through flywheels of commerce and information.

Like ecological systems, the greater the diversity of a B2B ecosystem, the greater resistance and resilience in the face of company, customer, partner, community, market disturbance, competition, or other unforeseen disruptive events.

In B2B ecosystems, cost and time is conserved.

Information flows through the system—typically from influence to commerce—while trust is recycled, preserved, and grown.

Where there are ecosystems in B2B, they should mirror systems of ecology. The reality is, ecosystems are everywhere.

They are base to life. And the more stable, the more they thrive.

In this new world, the currency isn't data.

The currency is trust.

A Crisis of Conviction

Trust is increasing in value. There's not a lot of it to be had these days. An undeniable shift, everywhere.

Trust in the old institutions like governments, major media, and official experts is waning. Trust in new tools and tech platforms is also waning. Trust in strangers is low.

What's that mean if you're a stranger to your customers, partners, or colleagues? To win a market, you have to be part of that market. You have to be known in that market. You have to be trusted in that market.

The crisis of trust is both a danger and an opportunity. Decreasing trust can cause people to tune out, go too far inward, retreat, shrink their networks, and reduce their world and the opportunities that come from a broader experience.

If they trust and get burned, they retreat further. That's the danger. But opportunity is there too. A crisis of trust isn't all bad. It's a needed correction to curb the excesses of The Infocalypse and abuses of power.

It brings some welcome discipline to markets and culture. In an increasingly virtual world, it demands the real. The human. The genuine.

It demands a lot out of your company too. But that will help you in the long run. No matter how strong your willpower and company culture, you will be shaped by the incentive structure you're in.

A world that doesn't trust easily forces you to be better.

Good.

Our Call to Action

PartnerHacker exists to create a world where everyone can succeed, to-gether. A mission whose time has come. And that's why I am so excited to launch PartnerHacker.com with my co-founder Isaac Morehouse and a great team.

Our goal is to be the #1 place for ideas, inspiration, news, and resources in the era of partner ecosystems.

Rather than duplicate or compete, we want to highlight the best and be a meta-resource that curates, connects, and comments on all the great stuff that's out there. We have deep conviction in this "partnerships moment." And it's not just us. Even the old guard is throwing away the old ways.

The author of arguably the most influential B2B sales book of the 2000s, The Challenger Sale, Brent Adamson recently published Traditional B2B Marketing and Sales are Becoming Obsolete.

And he didn't publish it on some no-name blog. This was published in Harvard Business Review (HBR). So what was Brent's prediction in HBR on the future of B2B sales and marketing?

- The future of B2B sales and marketing? An end to B2B sales and marketing. He didn't mince words.
- Why this shift? We'll say it again.

Trust is the new data

Data helped us automate and create efficiencies. Data helped us find, track, and target customers. But we're now awash in data and customers are exhausted by being served up algorithmically-determined content and crammed into impersonal funnels.

The noise is overwhelming the signal.

Customers are people. They have info fatigue. They are looking to trusted influencers and communities to help them make decisions and purchases. They want a seamless experience that fits the rhythms and patterns of their own lives, rather than being bombarded with attempts to fit them into a company's pipeline.

A partnerships and ecosystems approach is the remedy.

It has the power to combine the best of the digital world in all its scale and efficiency with the best of the organic, natural, human world of rich, deep, overlapping networks and nodes of trust.

PartnerHacker is here to cover, encourage, and nurture this transformation.

Welcome to the new world.

Where signal can rise above noise. Where relationships are required for action. Where trust is the new data.

This is our manifesto. A manifesto for the partnerships moment. Where we build robust, complex, and sustainable business ecosystems. Where we partner and win.

The Software Partnerships Series

By Sunir Shah

Sunir Shah is CEO at AppBind, and is president of the Cloud Software Association. AppBind makes it easy for partner resellers to buy your SaaS and bill their clients, and CSA is the SaaS Partnerships Network with over 4,000 SaaS partnership professionals.

This article was originally published on the CSA website.

Part One: Software Partnerships are Unpredictable Revenue

It's an open secret. Software-as-a-service (SaaS) partnerships are hard. In fact, they are a lot harder than most expect.

By requiring an ongoing direct relationship between customer and software maker, software companies are forced into direct sales and direct marketing, which leaves little room for partnerships.

Why the PC revolution grew faster than SaaS

The PC revolution was a big change to how software was made and sold. Before the eighties, software companies used to sell big enterprise licenses. They'd be happy to sell 1000 units, or perhaps win some kind of recurring service agreement associated with the software.

In the eighties, that changed when someone figured out you could put software in a box and ship it to retail. This meant that instead of 100-1000 units sold, some companies were selling hundreds of thousands of units. In fact, the fastest growing software company of the time was Lotus, which sold $53 million in the first year (about $125 million today).

That was the power of the channel in the PC revolution.

Even though Lotus did well, most software companies were losing money, and because of that, *InfoWorld*, the tech magazine, doubted the PC revolution.

Partnerships made the PC revolution

What I love about this story is it really shows the partnership role in software.

If you look back in 1983, when this *InfoWorld* article was published, the biggest software company was MicroPro International, not Microsoft.

MicroPro International made WordStar, the dominant word processing software of the early PC revolution. At their peak, **WordStar sold 700,000 units in one year by leveraging bundles**. This made their channel marketing strategy amazing. Their bundling deals with early personal computers such as Osborne computers meant whenever a computer was sold, WordStar was sold.

Lotus made a classic partnership mistake

Lotus, the fastest growing software company of the time, started as an overlooked team inside VisiCorp, the creator of the number one spreadsheet, VisiCalc. While VisiCorp was distracted with their success, Lotus began brokering a deal with IBM and committed to building Lotus for IBM OS/2.

But when Microsoft made a deal with IBM to build the operating system MS-DOS for the PC, Lotus did not adapt.

Eventually, their overcommitment to IBM OS/2 killed them.

Partnership dreams are BIG dreams

If you ever wanted to know why the value of partner people in software is so high, it's because partnership decisions are the ones that make and break software companies. Opportunities seized, platforms chosen, and options negotiated have a huge impact on a company's success.

Partner leaders dream of closing a deal that will be their company's breakout success, and they fear missing opportunities that will lead to a zeroed out future.

That's what the members of the Cloud Software Association believe in. We're the SaaS partnership network. We all want to close the $100 million partnership.

So, why aren't partnerships the most important team in SaaS?

While this may lead you to believe that partnerships should be the most important team at any cloud software company, we all know that the teams that grow the fastest are sales and customer success.

That's because of Predictable Revenue.

Predictable revenue is an effective strategy for predictably growing your revenue by consistently applying more sales labor. Hence, sales teams are always growing.

Partnerships are UNpredictable revenue. In partnerships, we're working with big wild bets, which means we don't have a process that guarantees results.

Moreover, a typical partnership person has to keep so many different partner channels open in their mind in a given week. From Monday at 9:00 a.m. to Friday at 5:00 p.m., those of us in partnerships and business development work on three or four completely different programs from resellers, to integrations, to distribution, to comarketing.

This is why we partnership leaders love the work, and why we love landing a deal.

Breaking through the growth ceiling of SaaS

As industry veterans know, there is a growth ceiling in B2B SaaS. Most companies struggle to get 10,000 companies to subscribe, let alone 100,000 companies.

This year, a few companies may break a million companies paying for their SaaS.

After years of partnership people, channel people, and reseller people coming to SaaS Connect trying to figure out how to get their distribution networks to work, we're now on the precipice.

It mirrors the same change that occurred in 1984, and just like they didn't really know if it would work out, we don't really know either.

I don't know about you, but I don't want 100,000 subscriptions. I want 1,000,000. Only the partner people can do that because we're the only ones who can set up distribution.

That's what the Cloud Software Association is all about. We're working together to build the market for cloud software distribution. It's a network of people who love that chaotic unpredictable revenue, with so many ideas in their heads. It's for people who want to figure out that distribution puzzle. It's for people who want to make the big deal that leads to 1,000,000 sales.

Part Two: A Framework to Understand All Software Partnerships

As we discussed before, partnerships can feel like unpredictable revenue. It can seem to some like there's no rhyme, nor reason to how partnerships work.

But we have learned some things about partnerships over the years, and I'm going to give you a little framework on how to think about partnerships

The 3 SaaS partnership revenue metrics

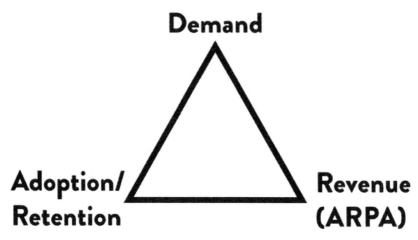

The KPIs to measure revenue of SaaS partnerships

There are three primary KPIs to measure partnership revenue:

1. **Demand driven.** Partnerships that get you more volume at the top of your funnel that

2. **Stickier adoption and retention.** While harder to track, it's critical to convince customers to adopt software and then keep using it. Partnerships help build a whole product solution that is more compelling to your customers.

3. **Higher average revenue per account (ARPA).** Upselling and cross-selling your customers on partner products and services increases the total money captured from each customer.

Every partnership deal you do can be analyzed by impacting one or maybe two of these metrics to see what the return on investment (ROI) might be.

The 3 partnership levers

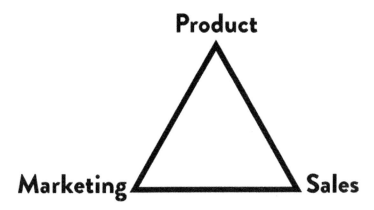

Software partnerships work by leveraging one of three dimensions of power.

An effective partnership leverages something the partner has in order to help you. If you've ever heard of the investment principle of leveraging "OPM" (Other People's Money), this is the same concept but for partnerships.

There are three principle levers in technical partnerships:

1. **Other people's product(s).** Building a whole product solution out of component parts. For instance, putting a CPU in a laptop, or integrating applications together.
2. **Other people's marketing.** Gaining distribution to a new or wider market through a partner's channel. For instance, app stores, referral sites like G2Crowd, or retail distribution like Staples.
3. **Other people's sales.** Having the partner resell your product to their customers. For instance, agencies and consultants, bundled cross-sales, or master/agent reseller channels.

The love triangle of SaaS

Unfortunately, the SaaS business model has a fundamental problem. The subscription billing model requires a customer to have a direct relationship with the software maker. After all, how do you create a recurring stream of payments without a direct contract between customer and software maker?

This forces SaaS into a direct sales and direct marketing model.

When a reseller or distributor gets between the customer and the software maker, it makes a love triangle, and the partner and the software maker fight over the customer. This creates a lot of friction building a distribution channel.

Conflict with your partners is a good way to snuff out a relationship. Not to mention, you can only create a channel if you are giving up room for others to create value around you.

To quote Bill Gates on what makes a platform work:

"A platform is when the economic value of everybody that uses it, exceeds the value of the company that creates it. Then it's a platform." — Bill Gates

Case in point: How the industry changed when the partnership levers changed

To understand the state of the software partnership market today, let's work through this model by comparing today to the PC market in the eighties.

PC product integrations were weak

In the PC world, product integration was pretty weak because it was really hard to do application-to-application data sharing. Product integration was primarily vertical: from the computer, to the operating system, to the application stack.

This very tight integration led to opportunities like WordStar being bundled with Osborne computers and Lotus being the killer app for the official IBM PC. Vertical integration sold a lot of units while horizontal partnerships between apps was very difficult.

PC software dominated because of resellers

Where the PC market really dominated was leveraging Other People's Sales with the reseller market. Resellers or value-added resellers (VARS), as we would call them, would buy the hardware and buy this new stuff called "independent software" from "independent software vendors" (ISVs) and stitch it together to build a complete solution to sell it on to end customers as their own product.

These ISVs made a great advance called the "software license" which was fundamental to the reseller channel's rapid growth. Software licenses let you put diskettes in a box and ship them through the retail distribution to all these shopping malls in America. It was a huge distribution network.

SaaS reseller partnerships are weak

But SaaS is different because it's very difficult to resell. After all, how do you resell a subscription? How do you put a subscription in a box and ship it? You can't.

Consequently, when working with resellers, most of us rely on a referral model, or an affiliate model (basically a referral model). Distribution is consequently typically referral-based. When you're looking at G2Crowd or GetApp or generating leads from app marketplaces, it's referral-based distribution rather than true resale.

Of course, referrals are much weaker than a resale distribution chain because the transactions are indirect, which creates an inefficient market and slower growth.

SaaS product integrations are strong

That there's a partner ecosystem in SaaS at all is because of product partnerships.

SaaS is really software on a network. Unlike the PC days, the network allows the data to be integrated, which allows us to create product-to-product integrations, which allows software companies to create a partner network from their integrations.

Interestingly, product integrations in SaaS are different than the PC days, where most integrations were component integrations. For instance, put a CPU in a laptop. That's great because you have a 100% market penetration because the CPUs are in every laptop.

SaaS is not like that. We have horizontal and indirect connections. We create a web of software so it's always a smaller conversion rate.

If you're finding your product integrations are not creating hockey-stick growth, it's because we're doing these side-to-side web of product integrations rather than a component/stack integration.

Indeed, if we want the market penetration of component integrations, the future of SaaS product integration may be more embeddable widgets.

Economics of reaching the shopping malls of America

Finally, the biggest difference in economic terms that led to the PC revolution was that the cost of software dropped by magnitudes. In the 1970s, Demand was low but Average Revenue Per Account was very high. If you sold 1,000 units each at tens of thousands of dollars, plus service contracts, you'd have a good company.

The PC revolution changed the equation. The top companies sold software at consumer prices because they prioritized maximizing demand through the retail distribution system.

This kind of channel strategy does not rely on a sales team strategy at all. It requires a partnership strategy.

Breaking the SaaS love triangle

The key lesson here is that the partnership strategy truly shines when there's a mechanism that allows the channel to create a "value chain" from the manufacturer to retail.

The future will require that we find a way to change SaaS to stop the channel conflict.

There might be an answer. Read the next part in the series.

Part Three: Breaking the SaaS Love Triangle

What is the SaaS love triangle?

As mentioned previously, SaaS creates a love triangle. Customers must subscribe to the software maker, which creates an ongoing relationship directly between the customer and the software maker.

This means when a partner like a reseller or a distributor is in between the customer and the software maker, the software maker is motivated to squeeze out their partner.

Both are fighting for the same customer. It's a love triangle, which is just as bad for business as it is for life.

Channel conflict slows growth

This channel conflict has kept growth rates of SaaS low. Last year, the global GDP of B2B SaaS was merely $46 billion. Yet Microsoft alone made $97 billion.

And Microsoft makes over 90% of its revenue from partners for the simple reason that they want partners to make eight times the revenue as Microsoft.

Microsoft is a global behemoth because it figured out how to create a global value chain around it, a value chain that is much larger than itself.

A reseller's snapshot of the PC software value chain

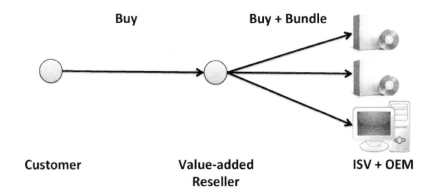

How did resellers build their business in the 1980s?

What Microsoft and its peers in the 1980s got really right was how to work with the companies that bought, sold, and supported software to end clients.

Indeed, almost all our partnership jargon today comes from the early 1980s. In the 1970s, it was common for hardware manufacturers to just include software as part of the product. However, the 1980s ushered in the era of "independent software vendors" (ISVs) who wrote software independently of the hardware companies.

These ISVs would work with consultants called value-added resellers (VARs) that were hired by end customers to build systems.

The VARs would buy and bundle hardware from Original Equipment Manufacturers (OEMs) and software from ISVs, then system-integrate

(SI) the lot into a much bigger whole product solution to solve a customer's unique problem, such as an office management system or a manufacturing process.

However, in the 21st century, this model has become much more difficult. It's very hard to buy and bundle software as a value-added reseller because customers must subscribe to the software maker directly.

While value-added resellers still try to stitch together integrated systems to solve business problems for their clients, the friction of not being able to buy the components of the system directly themselves has frustrated the reseller model.

A vision for a SaaS reseller value chain

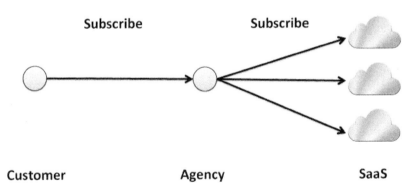

The future of how agencies will buy and sell subscriptions

Reselling subscription services is a different concept than reselling equipment. It may sound like a totally new model for software, but really, it's a very old model.

Consider the same problem but without computers. People hire agencies all the time to handle business operations such as accounting, marketing, logistics, maintenance and support, and so on.

These agencies, in turn, subcontract to other service providers to fulfill parts of the contract. For instance, they might hire bookkeepers, designers, lawyers, trades, and so on.

The future is to align with this model. A customer should be able to hire (i.e. subscribe to) an agency to run their sales, marketing, IT, dev ops, and so on. This agency should be able to hire (i.e. subscribe to) software services to fulfill their contract.

There are certainly agencies who do this already, such as managed service providers (MSPs), internet marketing agencies, and dev shops; however, they are struggling to juggle all the subscription accounting by hand.

The Complete Integrated Partnership Launch Checklist

By Sunir Shah

Sunir Shah is CEO at Appbind and is president of the Cloud Software Association. Appbind makes it easy for partner resellers to buy your SaaS and bill their clients, and CSA is the SaaS Partnerships Network with over 4,000 SaaS partnership professionals. A big thanks to Ronen Vengosh who provided his own partnership launch checklist for Egnyte.

This article was originally published on the CSA website.

Organize your partnership pipeline by stages

A partnership manager's job is to herd a partnership deal along. That means deciding what's relevant in a given moment.

When you organize your partnership pipeline by these stages, everything becomes a lot simpler. You can focus and prioritize your efforts on partners that are executing. You can organize your activities checklist by stage. And eventually, as you grow your team, you can delegate different stages to different team members.

Partnership launch stages

I have found that integrated partnerships best follow these stages, where each stage involves a different set of people to buy-in, such as the product team, engineering, marketing, sales, and support.

- **Target.** Potential partners you have yet to reach out to.
- **Handshaking.** Initial conversations. No plans yet.
- **Spec.** Specification of what the integration will look like.
- **Dev committed.** Engineer teams are allocated. This could be either party, or even a third-party agency.
- **QA.** Quality assurance of the integration.
- **Pre-launch.** Preparing for the marketing launch.
- **Launch!** The big day. Launching the integration to the market.
- **Post-launch.** Activities in the immediate aftermath of the launch.

Handshaking

At this stage, both partners are assessing if there is an opportunity. While persuading a partner to do a deal is an entire topic of conversation, in order to enter the next phase, you need to complete a few key actions:

- **Common vision.** You and your partner should share a common vision of how your companies can work together for the better service of customers, and thereby improve your marketability.

- **Identify target customers.** Your customer bases overlap imperfectly. Which customer types are you impacting?
- **Identify use cases.** What customer use cases are you going to solve (roughly)?
- **Assess market opportunity.** What kind of marketing will the partner do if you did an integration (roughly)?
- **Assess hot-to-trot-ness.** How excited and willing is your partner to do a deal?
- **Get technical documentation.** API docs and other technical information you need to build a spec.

Spec

If the partnership is worth exploring, the next step is to design the integration by looking at what is technically possible and by asking potential customers what they want. This may be delegated to a product team or your partner.

- **Customer research.** Email, phone, survey potential customers to capture the use cases.
- **Product specification.** Some kind of implementation plan of how the integration will work.
- **Review and accept spec.** Review the spec with the stakeholders of the partnership to confirm you can move forward.

Dev committed

Once the spec is accepted, engineering needs to be committed and scheduled. Be careful as engineering teams are often reallocated from partnerships.

- **Schedule work.** When is the project expected to begin?
- **Spec review.** Review the spec with the product manager or engineering team lead before they break ground. This also serves to confirm they will break ground.

Quality assurance

Make sure the integration works by testing it internally and externally.

- **Personal smoke test.** You should personally try the integration to make sure it works as expected and to make sure you understand it.
- **Internal Quality Assurance.** Have someone else inside your company try the integration and look for problems.
- **Beta testers.** Recruit actual customers, often those you talked to during customer research, to try it out and confirm it.
- **Beta reviews and case studies.** Get feedback, testimonials, reviews, and case studies from your beta customers that you can use in your sales and marketing collateral.
- **Partner Quality Assurance.** Let your partner do QA if they want to.

Pre-launch

Get organized before launch day. Many teams will be impacted by an integration. It's your responsibility to prepare them.

Core assets

Some assets you will need over and over again, so get them ready.

- **Logo.** Both vector and bitmap forms.
- **Integration elevator pitch.** What problem does the integration solve and how?
- **Company elevator pitch.** What problem does your product solve and how?
- **Description.** What pains do you solve? What benefits do you offer? What's your position against your competitors?
- **Screenshots.** Pick screenshots that sell.
- **Explainer video.** Make a marketing video that sells your product and the integration.
- **Walk-through screencast.** Make a video that explains how to set up and use the integration.
- **Tracking links.** What UTMs, referral links, or landing pages are you going to use to track customers?

Pre-launch for support

Support is going to take the brunt of technical problems with the integration. Make sure they know how it works, what problem it is solving, and how to reach you to escalate problems.

- **Support contact information.** Exchange contact information between support teams. If you can, not only what can be publicly shared with customers, but also a direct contact between the support teams to escalate issues quickly.
- **Service-level agreements.** Is there a support service-level agreement? Which support team is responsible for what?
- **Help center article.** Include the elevator pitch for the integration and the overall description. Explain how to enable and use the integration. Address Frequently Asked Questions that came up during beta testing. Include the screenshots and the walk-through screencast.
- **Webinar (internal).** Do a webinar or video call to demo the integration for the support team.

Pre-launch for sales

A common mistake is thinking that your partner's sales team will sell your product to their customers. This will be your big break, you think. And then, of course, they don't.

Sales people do not sell partner products; their job is to sell their core product. They will only use partner products if it helps them overcome an objection to selling their core product. Make sure you can help them with that by asking them what objections they are facing and seeing how you can overcome them.

- **Elevator pitch for the integration.** In two sentences, what customer problem are you solving with the integration and how? What is your unique value proposition? What sales problem are you solving with the integration?

- **Elevator pitch for your product.** In two sentences, what customer problem are you solving with your company?
- **One-pager.** Sales loves one-pagers they can "shoot over" to customers that answer most questions so they don't have to. If you have case studies from your beta customers, include them. Social proof is key.
- **Explainer video.** If they won't read your one-pager, they will watch the explainer video.
- **Webinar (internal).** Do a webinar or video call to demo the integration for the sales team and explain how it will help them sell more.
- **Sales tracking.** Will customers interested in the integration be tagged in the CRM?

Pre-launch for marketing

To make the launch work efficiently, you need to prepare all your marketing communications before launch. Make sure your partner agrees and coordinates with their marketing communications team to deliver these early in the partnership. Usually you reciprocate.

- **Schedule.** When are you going to "launch" the integration? Meaning, when is the marketing push?
- **Blog post.** Are they writing a blog post selling and explaining the integration to their customers? Do they need the elevator pitch and description, explainer video, screenshots, tracking links, case studies?
- **Landing page.** Are you designing special landing pages?

- **Directory/app store listing.** Do they have an integrations directory? Do you need copy, screenshots, explainer videos, support contact information, tracking links, reviews from beta customers, case studies?
- **Social media mentions.** What will they push on social media? The explainer video, screenshots, link to the landing page, or link to the blog post?
- **Webinar.** Are you hosting a webinar for customers to talk through the integration?
- **Social media advertising.** Are you buying social media ads for the integration? What's the target? The landing page, blog, or webinar?
- **Newsletter.** What is the newsletter copy? Do they need the elevator pitch and description, explainer video, screenshots, tracking links, case studies, link to the webinar?
- **In-app messaging.** Will they announce the integration in their app, through in-app notifications or, if decided in the spec, directly in the user interface?
- **Drip email.** Are you designing a specialized drip campaign for new customers of that integration?
- **Press release.** Are you putting out a press release? Whose PR agency is coordinating? How much time do they need? What is the real story here? Do you need the elevator pitch and description, explainer video, screenshots, quotes from executives, case studies?

Launch!

On launch day, it's time to flip the switch on the integration and push out all the marketing communications. Your job is to get the team engaged to deal with any problems and take advantage of any opportunities.

- Remind support. Remind support you're launching so they are prepared.
- Confirm with product. Confirm with product they can release the integration to the public.
- Confirm with marketing. Confirm with marketing they are ready to launch the communications.
- Confirm with partner. Confirm with partner they are ready to launch the communications.
- Go! Flip the switch.
- Watch the results. Keep an eye on customer channels, social media, and the support queue to react to any problems or opportunities.

After the launch

You're not done yet. To maximize the opportunity, you need to keep developing the momentum.

- **Report the results.** Your partner wants to know if it worked too.
- **Solicit customer feedback, reviews, case studies.** Contact customers using the integration while they are still excited.

- **Do a post-mortem.** Talk to your partner about what worked and didn't. Identify any further opportunities.
- **Schedule future calls.** Stay in touch with your partners to both learn of opportunities they have and offer marketing opportunities to them to keep them engaged.

Partnerships take time. Continue with ongoing market development activities:

- Blog posts
- Webinars
- Attend, sponsor, speak at partner conferences
- Co-sponsor cocktail parties at trade shows
- Write a whitepaper or ebook together
- Buy advertisements about the integration (PPC, retargeting)
- Channel marketing to their or your channel partners, including case studies, customer reviews, and any partner programs you offer

And of course, keep building better use cases through ongoing product activities:

- Continually improve quality
- Find new use cases to integrate
- Keep up with new APIs or product opportunities; offer to be a beta customer of new APIs

Work towards being offered directly in the partner's user interface.

Platform + Ecosystem

By Avanish Sahai

Avanish Sahai is a Tidemark Fellow and board member at Hubspot; he's a former platform ecosystem leader at Salesforce, ServiceNow, and Google.

Articles originally published on Tidemark.

Part One: The Way

Successful software companies are increasingly developing and promoting a platform strategy that allows them to expand their footprint, deliver greater customer value, and capture increased share of wallet.

This entails building both a product strategy and framework (e.g. exposing and maintaining APIs and/or platform-as-a-service [PaaS] capabilities) as well as building an ecosystem of developers and independent software vendors (ISVs) that can extend the platform and application offerings with their own expertise to deliver more complete customer solutions.

Examples of companies that have effectively done this include Atlassian, HubSpot, Salesforce, ServiceNow, and many others. The platform decision is a product strategy and investment decision that generally precedes the decision to build an ecosystem of partners to leverage the platform.

Technology companies that identify and act on a platform opportunity are able to sustain higher growth rates and valuations. This requires assessing what type of platform and ecosystem opportunities may exist, and making the right investments in tech, go-to-market, and other key resources to capture the opportunity.

In this article, we will explore winning strategies for building such platform strategies and associated ecosystems.

What is a platform?

There are different ways to think about being a platform. For our purposes, we are defining a platform as a construct that allows a company's offering to be extended rapidly through "extending with or building on top of" the core offering.

There can be many different levels and tiers, but this is a simple starting point. Not every company can or should be a platform.

Certain offerings, based on the problems they're solving and how they're architected, have more of a "right" to be a platform.

Why are platforms becoming more prominent?

The most successful companies in the current era are platform companies.

In fact, six of the ten most valuable companies are platform companies, including Apple, Microsoft, Alphabet, Amazon, Facebook, and Tencent. Interestingly, many of these companies are less than 25 years old. This means that relatively young companies have achieved trillions in market value by pursuing a platform strategy. Even Apple and Microsoft, which were founded in 1976, have grown substantially faster after adopting a more open platform mindset; Apple with the iPhone and Microsoft with the Windows ecosystem, and now Azure and Xbox.

Platform companies grow bigger and faster. Considering growth from a revenue perspective, platform companies hit $1 billion, $10 billion faster than other types of companies. Again, Microsoft is a great example of how embracing a platform strategy can lead to explosive growth.

What is an ecosystem?

An ecosystem is a way for platform companies to drive more value to customers and to drive more customers to the platform. In the process, companies can capture greater market share and share of wallet. In tech, platform companies have a large cadre of developers or other supporting teams that specialize in delivering products or applications tailored to the operating system of the platform.

Think of the iPhone and its ecosystem of apps. The more apps a customer installs, the more entrenched they become in the ecosystem and platform, creating a virtuous cycle between the customer, the core device, and the model. This approach also has the benefit of creating network effects. The more apps a customer or their friends use, the more adoption grows, which leads to opportunities for aggregated monetization, merchandising, and so forth.

Companies can use a platform + ecosystem approach as a lever to help sustain their growth rate long-term. Consider the track record of two platform and ecosystem vanguards, Salesforce and HubSpot. The following charts showcase their LTM revenue growth ($ quantum increase quarter-over-quarter, as well as the % YoY growth rate). Both businesses have been able to consistently increase their LTM revenue, in part due to their platform and ecosystem strategy.

Salesforce, for example, ramped up revenue monetization of their ecosystem in 2010, after initially launching the AppExchange in 2005. The monetization approach brought greater value to partners through improved marketing and field alignment, which created demand from customers (and thus drove stickiness and increased penetration for Salesforce's own offerings).

HubSpot LTM Revenue QoQ Growth ($ Amount) and
LTM Revenue YoY Growth Rate (%)

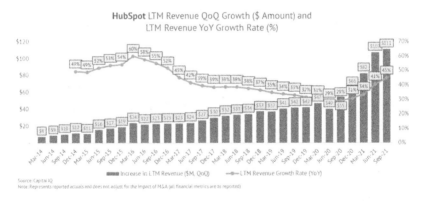

Source: Capital IQ
Note: Represents reported actuals and does not adjust for the impact of M&A (all financial metrics are as reported)

Since HubSpot went public, the company has demonstrated consistent growth north of 30%, with a recent acceleration of growth in part due to their success moving to a multi-product strategy (marketing automation, customer service product suite, sales force automation, content management, etc.).

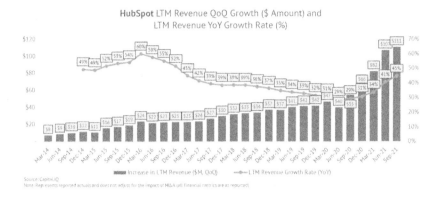

HubSpot LTM Revenue QoQ Growth ($ Amount) and
LTM Revenue YoY Growth Rate (%)

What are the drawbacks of not pursuing a platform strategy?

Non-platform companies generally have slower growth rates and also face higher costs to vertically integrate their offerings and "build it all in house."

There are many examples of non-platform companies across industry sectors, including retail (Walmart) and industrial manufacturing (GE, Siemens). Instead of pursuing a platform strategy or adopting open integration approaches, they have typically tried to provide complete hardware and software solutions.

Companies may have very good reasons to remain closed and not expose their API to external developers, but the opportunity costs to growth and market share seem clear.

Questions to ask yourself when considering a platform

There are different approaches to creating a platform depending on the problem you are solving, and it is possible for a company to fit into more than one approach. In the beginning, look for one good entry point and expand to others over time.

Ask these questions as you consider becoming a platform:

- Am I making it easy to do something?

Consider how Stripe and Twilio provide API-based access to accelerate key functions like payments or messaging, respectively.

- Do I have a lot of data that is valuable?

Are you collecting data that is incredibly valuable and can serve as a system of record for others to leverage? Good examples of platforms operating in this way include ServiceNow and HubSpot.

- Can you automate a broader process and, by doing so, significantly drive more value?

You are building and automating a business process by connecting various apps to a core. Salesforce is a good example of this platform approach.

While not for everybody, having a platform vision can help companies grow faster and achieve higher valuations than they could have achieved otherwise.

A platform vision requires a thoughtful approach to defining what the "platform strategy" for a specific company would mean, embedding that mindset into the company's DNA, and having a clear execution plan to build it out.

With these core concepts established, our next pieces will look at the what and the how of building a software platform and ecosystem.

Part Two: What Does It Mean to Be a Platform + Ecosystem Company?

What are the various types of platforms for tech companies?

In the tech sector, "platform" can mean many different things. Here, we define some common platform approaches and historical examples:

- **APIs:** Expose Application Programming Interfaces (APIs) to enable certain functions to be done quickly and easily (hiding the complexity from the developers). Examples include Twilio delivering Messaging APIs and Stripe for Payment APIs.

- **Common data models:** Creating a "standard" definition of certain objects/content that becomes widely accepted and adopted. Examples include ServiceNow's implementation of the Configuration Management Database (CMDB) for IT Assets and Services and Salesforce's pioneering standardization of Contacts and Accounts for sales data.

- **Integrated Workflows:** The ability to quickly and easily connect application flows while sharing underlying data/data models to create a more seamless experience. Salesforce's

Lightning App Builder and ServiceNow's Now Platform accomplish this.

- **Platform as a Service:** A holistic offering that enables developers to rapidly build applications by leveraging pre-built underlying services. AWS Elastic Beanstalk, Google App Engine, and Salesforce's Heroku are examples.
- **Infrastructure as a Service:** Core infrastructure capabilities (databases, networking, and security) that can be used as
- building blocks to create the underlying stack on which applications can be built, providing greater control and flexibility to developers. Examples include Google Compute Engine and the core Amazon Web Services.
- **App Marketplaces:** Offerings that expose any combination of the above to enable customers to discover, purchase, and install apps and integrations aligned with a certain platform. Salesforce AppExchange and Microsoft Azure Marketplace are examples.

These platform approaches are not mutually exclusive. Many companies provide a "mix and match" of multiple platform capabilities. Think about where you sit in the spectrum of platforms and where you see your users and customers engage. This can help you to determine the right mix of capabilities.

The journeys of companies with successful platforms

Looking at the journeys of companies with successful platforms offers valuable insights into how a platform strategy can evolve over time.

Salesforce: App -> Multiapp -> Platform

Salesforce launched with Sales Force Automation (SFA) software. Over time, the company added applications for customer service and marketing. Underlying these applications was a common data framework around the customer. A natural step was to build a platform layer on/around the core applications to enable extensions of use cases and workflows.

ServiceNow: Platform -> App -> Multiapp + Platform

ServiceNow started out as a cloud platform in 2004 but was a cloud platform before its time. The team then went back to the drawing board and built an application for IT Service Management (ITSM) which allowed it to flourish.

They later expanded that application for other components of IT services, including operations and monitoring, creating a billion-dollar business. Now, with incredible traction, they have returned to their platform roots, supporting the development of a range of Workflow applications for IT, Employees, and Customers, built on top of their core cloud platform and integrating with hundreds of other tools and apps, all exposed via their marketplace, the ServiceNow Store.

Hubspot: App -> Multiapp - > Platform

HubSpot started as the "go-to" application for inbound, content-driven marketing. Based on the success of this offering, the company has since expanded into Sales and Customer Service, as well as content management and operations for SMB and mid-market customers. HubSpot, based on customer demand, has also built a substantial partner ecosystem that allows for customers to easily extend the core applications with offerings from partners. (Disclosure: the author sits on the HubSpot Board of Directors.)

Amazon/AWS: Retail App -> Infrastructure Platform

Amazon famously started as a retail application and remained so for its first decade or so. While its retail app has become ubiquitous, many people may be surprised to learn that most of the company's profits now come from its platform, an infrastructure Amazon offers to others to build on top of it—Amazon Web Services.

Many applications and websites today run on AWS, and its infrastructure services have grown into a $60 billion business.

Apple: iPhone -> App Store/Ecosystem

Apple's iPhone is a gold standard example of how a successful platform can create network effects. The more apps created, the stickier the platform becomes, and it helps to drive adoption and create opportunities for aggregated merchandise, infrastructure service, and more.

Atlassian: Multi App (via M&A) -> Marketplace for Developers

Atlassian started out in Australia with developer-oriented products like Jira and Confluence. Over time, it acquired numerous other products/companies (Bitbucket, Trello, etc.) and has become the de facto standard for in-house developers and software engineers to manage their development processes. It has since built a thriving marketplace where third-party developers can list their offerings and seamlessly sell their wares to Atlassian customers with pre-built integration hooks. This marketplace has resulted in over $1 billion in sales, with the developer community aggregating most of the value.

What we learn from these journeys

These examples underscore the myriad of entry points to a platform strategy. Going a level deeper, each type of platform brings a different set of decision-making requirements and tradeoffs.

What are the investment requirements? What will the go-to-market for the platform look like? Who will the primary customer/user target personas be?

Adopting a platform strategy requires alignment among decision-making entities across the company. For boards, pursuing a platform is a core element of a company's strategy. Platforms require investment and patience; becoming

a platform doesn't happen overnight. Internally, it is critical for teams like product, marketing, sales, partnerships, channels, etc. to have a shared understanding of what it means to be a platform. For example, there needs to be clarity on how to handle conflicts and how partner programs are built and executed.

Equally important is the ecosystem. Stakeholders need to have confidence in the platform from a quality, investment, and access perspective. It is also important to have acceptance within the ecosystem—a platform vendor, or orchestrator may become a competitor at some point.

Once these internal and external components are aligned, how do you recruit partners to build on top of your platform and create value for your users? We will explore these strategic elements in our third article. Stay tuned!

Platform + Ecosystem Players Consistently Outperform

Platform + ecosystem players have consistently outperformed the broader market as shown in the below charts detailing the performance of platform indices vs. the S&P and NASDAQ over various time horizons.

Stock Indices Performance (% Return): Since 2010

Part Three: How to Start, Scale, and Think About Your Platform + Ecosystem

What should you ask yourself as you consider how to build a platform + ecosystem strategy?

There are many key questions you should address as you consider your platform + ecosystem strategy. While answers vary by situation, tackling these questions upfront will help you build your platform + ecosystem fit for your purpose.

- Who are the primary users?
- Will they use the offerings internally or expose them externally?
- Is there an API strategy in place?
- What's the API management approach?
- What types of documentation are required?
- Do they need a development environment? Yours or theirs?
- What other systems/data do you need to coexist with?
- What type of packaging/distribution do they require (e.g., a Marketplace or an OEM strategy)?
- What's the business model/monetization strategy?
- Who's doing the billing? Metering it?
- Who owns the data?
- What limitations will be set on partners?

Once you have answers to the above questions, you'll want to consider what requirements and success look like for each type of platform strategy.

Consider the following approaches, which build on each other in terms of their sophistication and complexity.

If your platform...

1. **Makes it easy to do something**

    -   Define the audience very clearly. Identify if you will support internal developers or enable third-party partners, e.g., System Integrators (SIs).

    -   Create a clear API strategy. What are the APIs that you'll expose? How will they be maintained? What levels of documentation and sample code will you provide?

    -   This approach also requires you to invest in hiring tech-savvy internal teams to support developers and be very engaged with that community.

    -   To measure success, focus on (a) adoption rates of the offering by key constituents, e.g., developers, and (b) ultimately tracking monetization strategies (how they make money and share money with you).

2. **Gives access to valuable data**

    -   The audiences, in this case, may expand from developers and SIs to include other software vendors (ISVs) who may be building complementary offerings alongside your complete product and are looking to extend their offerings through your ecosystem.

- In addition to a clear API strategy, this approach often requires clarity of thinking about the organization's overall product strategy because it carries the potential for conflict. What happens if developers or ISVs build something that may compete with your plans? How are you communicating product roadmaps? If you are going to compete with your partners, how are you identifying and communicating changes that may threaten the ecosystem?

- The required skill sets for this approach change because it is not just you selling your offering. You and your partner are selling offerings that use common underlying data and help your customer solve a more complex problem. You'll need to invest in a team that can help position, recruit, onboard, build, and develop potential go-to-market (GTM) models with the partner ecosystem. How do you and your partners sell together? How do you educate the market? Also, consider the different needs of developers, from a self-sufficient one to an ISV or SI that may require much more sophisticated documentation and programs to adopt your data/technology.

- Measure success by how often end customers are adopting the combined solutions that you and partners are delivering. Track the type of revenue retention and growth the joint offering can drive. This is an important metric to monitor because, as we have consistently seen, businesses that have partner + ecosystem attached outperform net retention by 10%+.

3. **Builds a flywheel (by automating a process and driving more value)**

- In this case, the priority audiences are typically ISVs and SIs, rather than developers, that build around the core platform and extend it, helping to create a seamless experience for the end customer.

- Here, you'll have fully built out an integrated workflow, making the alignment of product roadmaps even more critical than in the second scenario. Workflows that integrate and work together will invariably become apps. It's then a question of who is building those new or complementary apps and how broad the "gray zone" is between the platform provider and their ecosystem partners.

- This more complex approach to a platform + ecosystem has the highest potential of creating conflict and confusion in the marketplace. It's essential to have a very clear product roadmap that demonstrates your understanding of all the elements of who your potential partners are, how you may benefit or compete with them, and how you think about it in terms of resourcing and product engagement.

- There is a definite need for a recruiting effort with ISVs and SIs. Generally, you'll find an expectation that combined offerings will be available through marketplaces or other similar distribution mechanisms. It's also important to define how your ecosystem will maintain confidentiality with respect to data sharing and partnerships.

- Success is measured through joint development, joint selling activities, and often a revenue share between the partners and the platform provider, which helps defray various development and joint GTM program costs.

Regardless of the approach you take to building your platform + ecosystem, a common denominator of all types is the cross-functional engagement model within your organization. No single team can figure it out in a silo. Creating a platform + ecosystem involves product, engineering, marketing, etc. These teams need to collaborate in terms of resourcing, defining explicit dependencies, and investments.

Another point to keep in mind is that building a platform + ecosystem is a long-term play. Even at the board level, it should be thought of as an investment and not an initiative to deliver immediate returns or replace your core sales and marketing efforts. Think in terms of years for the build-out. For example, a three-year plan could include Year 1 - build the platform, Year 2 - gain early adopters, Year 3 - scale to potential monetization.

As you hone in on your build-out plan, here are some common questions that can help to narrow in on where you need to focus your cross-functional alignment:

- **What are the investment and return time horizons?**

   Developing the platform strategy and the recruitment and onboarding of developers/ISVs/SIs is a long cycle and requires a sustained effort that will not yield immediate results.

- **What resources and commitments are required to execute?**

  Building a platform and ecosystem strategy is, by definition, a cross-functional effort. Thus, technical, resourcing, and business dependencies across teams (R&D, marketing, sales & pre-sales, partnerships) must be identified, funded, and tracked.

- **What are the key milestones and checkpoints?**

  Throughout the extended cycle described above, there needs to be a program management mindset that tracks progress across all functions and adjusts expectations and requirements to reflect the state of the offerings, market requirements, competitive landscapes, etc.

What I find most exciting about building a platform + ecosystem is that there isn't a one-size-fits-all approach. In this article, I've endeavored to capture the basics as a starting point as a resource for organizations looking to create their platform + ecosystem approach.

As you think of your unique situation, it is helpful to draw from the many excellent examples of companies that have navigated different approaches to building successful platform + ecosystem businesses.

The author would like to thank David Yuan and Phil James at Tidemark for their sponsorship and contributions to this series. Also, much gratitude to JZ Rigney and Katie Curnutte at Kingston Marketing Group for their terrific collaboration.

The Platform Matrix: Not All Platforms Are Created Equal

By Sameer Singh

Sameer Singh is a Network Effects Advisor and Investor, part of the Atomico Angel Program.

Multi-purpose platforms with native apps are much more scalable and defensible than focused platforms reliant on integrations.

Network effects shape three broad types of tech businesses—marketplaces, interaction networks, and data networks.

In addition to these, there is one other type of business where network effects play a central role—platforms. Unfortunately, the tech and startup world has spent much of the past decade using the term "platform" to describe everything from operating systems to analytics tools, algorithms, APIs, etc. Quite plainly, if everything is a platform, then nothing is, and the term loses all meaning.

Let's take a granular look at what platforms really are, and then unpack how their network effects work.

What is a platform?

The most meaningful definition of a platform comes from none other than Bill Gates, the architect of one of the first true platform businesses.

"A platform is when the economic value of everybody that uses it, exceeds the value of the company that creates it"

— Bill Gates (as relayed by Chamath Palapithiya)

Focusing on economic value to external participants automatically eliminates the vast majority of companies that call themselves platforms. For example, Tableau is a data visualization and analytics tool but not a platform. However, Xbox, iOS, Android, Salesforce, Shopify, and even Roku are all platforms because they help third-party developers generate economic value on top of their businesses.

In order to unlock this economic value, aspiring platforms need to have the following components:

1. Underlying product

Platforms are always built on top of an existing product with some standalone value. For example, iOS and Android were smartphone operating systems that had self-contained features (phone, text, web browser, etc.) even before developer activity took off.

2. Development framework

One of the most basic requirements for any platform is that it must allow third-party developers to leverage the platform's capabilities to create software products for platform users.

3. Matching

Modern platforms create an avenue for developers to distribute apps and help platform users discover apps that meet their needs. Enabling discovery is especially important because platforms own the primary relationship with customers or users.

4. Economic benefit

Finally, platforms provide economic benefits to developers and help them build, monetize, or enhance their businesses on top of the platform. These benefits can be either direct (earning revenue from the platform) or indirect (improving engagement or retention via the platform).

In summary, platforms combine an underlying product and the development capabilities of software frameworks with the matching and monetization functions of marketplaces.

Platform = Underlying Product + Development Capabilities + Marketplace

As a result, platforms have some similarities with marketplaces. For example, customer and developer fragmentation is critical for them to be viable. Also, platforms have **cross-side network effects,** i.e., the addition of each developer makes the platform more valuable for all users and vice versa. This feedback loop makes them more valuable as user and developer adoption grows.

Now that we understand the basics of platforms, let's take a deeper look at how platform network effects work.

Scalability: Platform Focus

I previously evaluated the scalability of marketplaces based on the geographic range of their network effects, i.e., the maximum physical distance between demand and supply for interactions to take place. Marketplaces with cross-border network effects are significantly more scalable than hyperlocal ones because they can leverage a supplier in one region to attract demand in another. However, we cannot use this approach to compare the relative scalability of platforms because they are purely digital businesses, i.e., their network effects are almost always cross-border. The addition of a developer in one region makes the platform more valuable for users all over the world, and vice versa.

If platforms are cross-border by nature, their scaling potential should depend on their ability to organically expand into adjacent vertical markets or categories (not regions). In other words, scalability depends on the **breadth of the platform's standalone capabilities.**

Take Xbox as an example—the underlying capabilities of the platform (processing power, graphics, controller) were designed for gaming. This focus and a growing base of game developers led to strong customer adoption, primarily from gamers. With the launch of the Xbox One,

Microsoft attempted to expand this gaming platform to a larger market—home entertainment. However, media was a small minority of the platform's value for its customer base. In addition, the Xbox One could not justify its price premium over competing streaming devices to non-gamers as its unique capabilities and developer base did not appeal to that market. As a result, Xbox could not expand their market or gain market share against other dedicated streaming devices.

Game consoles and entertainment platforms like Roku are the clearest examples of focused platforms, but they are not the only ones. In recent years, there have been a number of specialized SaaS tools that have launched their own developer programs and app stores. This includes Slack, Zoom, Okta, and Zendesk. They still meet the definition of platforms, but their developer programs are largely restricted to the specific use case of the underlying product.

This means that the most scalable platforms are those that are **multipurpose,** with capabilities that can enable a wide array of potential use cases.

Both iOS and Android (combined with Google Play) are great examples here. As smartphone operating systems, they have always enabled a wide variety of functions. For example, the first iPhone and the T-Mobile G1 (the first Android smartphone) both launched with roughly 15 pre-loaded apps, including YouTube and maps. As a result, they attracted customers who used them as multi-purpose platforms. This initial customer base, combined with a rapidly expanding collection of APIs, then helped them attract developers across a range of different categories, from gaming to social media, e-commerce, health, finance, and so on. In other words, they leveraged their capabilities to enter adjacent categories and evolve from mobile computing platforms to general-purpose computing platforms.

Multi-purpose platforms are not limited to computing. SaaS tools like Salesforce and Shopify have become essential infrastructure for their customers' operations and effectively act as operating systems for business. This allows them to create scalable, multi-purpose developer platforms as well.

Defensibility: Role of Developers

The defensibility of a marketplace is a function of how differentiated its supply is. Marketplaces with commoditized or interchangeable supply (like Uber) are less defensible (see higher multi-tenanting) and face more competition. Unfortunately, this framework is not directly applicable here either because all platforms have varying degrees of differentiated supply. Users look for apps that meet specific and varied needs, and they cannot automatically be substituted for one another. However, platforms are still vulnerable to competition and multi-tenanting, i.e., developers can use more than one platform. The scale of this risk depends on the importance of the platform to a developer's business.

Take Slack for example. Slack's app directory includes a range of apps that customers can use to improve their experience. However, the vast majority of popular apps are not actually "native," i.e., built on top of Slack from scratch.

Rather, they are **"connections"** or **"integrations"** to pre-existing apps.

The motivation for these developers is to make it easier for customers to use their apps in any context, i.e., **improving their UX.** For example, Asana is one of the most popular Slack integrations and allows users to convert Slack messages into tasks on Asana or link Asana projects to specific Slack channels. This makes it much more convenient for both Asana and Slack customers. However, this also means that developers are motivated to integrate their apps with any product that their customers use frequently. In addition, the platform is not a necessity for their app to exist, and it is relatively simple to extend "connections" to other platforms. This leads to **extensive multi-tenanting.** For example, Asana is also available on Microsoft Teams, Hangouts Chat, Glip, and Flock. And, of course, connectors like Zapier enable integration with even more collaboration tools.

In addition, "long tail" developers are less important since integrations are meant to **complement** the use case of the underlying product (and not create new use cases). As a result, competing platforms only need to have integrations with the most popular apps to create a "good enough" alternative. This isn't to say that these integrations don't create some switching costs—customers would need to set up all of their integrations again if they switch platforms. However, the wide availability of popular integrations **reduces barriers to switching** and weakens defensibility. Both Slack and Zoom rely on "connections" or "integrations" rather than **native apps**. Luckily, Slack has other forms of network effects that insulate it against competition. Unfortunately, Zoom does not.

In contrast, Salesforce is an example of a platform that skews towards native apps over integrations. Salesforce acts as a single source of truth, recording data about customer interactions and business operations. Developers leverage its capabilities and record data to build new, native apps that **extend the functionality** of the platform.

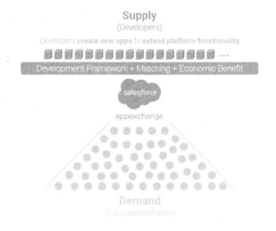

The motivation for developers here is to **target new market opportunities and acquire new customers.** Take Vlocity for example—it built a billion-dollar business by creating customized, industry-specific solutions on top of Salesforce. This extended the use cases of Salesforce's platform to areas as diverse as claims management in insurance and subscriber management in media streaming. Crucially, it was exclusively built on Salesforce. Vlocity would need to rebuild their application from scratch if they wanted to reach customers using another CRM. This acts as a **barrier to multi-tenanting** and limits competition.

Clearly, "long tail" developers are exceptionally important here because the whole point of these developer programs is to create functionality that the platform cannot build itself. As a result, competitors need to match the scale of the incumbent platform to provide a comparable experience. This makes network effects exceptionally strong, with first movers locking out later competition. For example, iOS and Android were first to create network effects between developers and smartphone users, which doomed late movers like Windows Phone. While there is extensive multi-tenanting between iOS and Android, this is because they were both essentially first movers targeting different market segments—Android's modular approach allowed it to penetrate markets that iOS simply could not reach.

The Platform Matrix: Extreme Outcomes

As we have done previously, we can now plot defensibility and scalability against each other to create a framework for evaluating platform network effects.

This shows a remarkable pattern that is effectively an inverse of the catch-22 we saw with data network effects. The majority of platforms are either both scalable and defensible, or neither.

The cause of this pattern is simple. Multi-purpose platforms create more opportunities for developers to discover new use cases, which leads to a larger market for native apps. This also creates exceptionally strong and defensible network effects as the value of the platform continues to grow with user and developer adoption. This is not only true for iOS, Android, and Salesforce, but also for Shopify, WeChat's Mini Programs, and even Atlassian.

On the other hand, the limited capabilities of focused platforms restrict new market opportunities and constrain native app development. These platforms have significantly weaker network effects but do create some switching costs. On the flip side, they are much easier to build because the use cases and complements already exist. Roku, Zendesk, Okta, and RingCentral fall into this category in addition to Slack and Zoom.

Building a platform is rarely a near-term option for early-stage startups because attracting third-party developers requires some level of scale.

However, by the time that scale is achieved, it is too late to choose the type of platform you want to build. At that point, the capabilities of the underlying product are already defined. If building a platform is the eventual goal, its desired capabilities need to be the core philosophy guiding your long-term product roadmap right from the start.

Strategic Alliances: PartnerUp and Play to Win

By Jared Fuller

Jared Fuller is the co-founder of PartnerHacker and co-host of

the PartnerUp podcast.

The root of strategic alliances is strategy. Strategy is choice. If you are playing to win, you must understand what strategy actually means: Not all choices are equal.

"You idiot, the KGB is here!"

I barely heard the whisper in my ear through the crowd when a dozen colleagues rushed me out the door and threw me into a car. We sped off.

I thought it was a joke.

"What do you mean, the KGB? Like, Stalin's KGB?" I yelled at my colleagues-turned-captors.

"Of course Stalin's KGB...Your joke about the President, you can NEVER make a joke about him here. We might not have seen you again. They were waiting for you to say something stupid, then BAM, black bag, and you would've been gone."

They weren't laughing.

I was in Minsk, the capital city of Belarus, speaking to a few hundred techies on how to build sales and partnerships.

If you've seen the PartnerHacker tagline, Trust is the New Data, or read the opening chapter of the Handbook, you'll find this ironic: Trust was the subject of the joke in question.

It went like this:

"According to a Harvard study, only 3% of people trust salespeople. Co-incidentally, about 3% of the population are also salespeople. I also hear that's about the same as Lukashenko's approval rating."

I smirked.

When I said it, a roar of laughter erupted, immediately followed by pin-drop silence. I touched a nerve, or two.

Back then, Minsk was the home of PandaDoc, and though both founders immigrated to the States, the tech team HQ still called Belarus home.

It was 2016. I was leading partnerships for PandaDoc, and the very next day, the C-suite of HubSpot was flying to Minsk to meet the PandaDoc engineering team.

We were in due diligence.

That next day would mark the biggest day of all of our lives.

That was one year, almost to the day, after my first conversation with that executive.

On that first call, I told him,

"In less than one year, I am going to be your number one partner globally, and you are going to try to buy me."

I made that promise from an apartment which served as our San Francisco office and, for a few months, my temporary bedroom.

The guts!

We were nobody. I was nobody.

Little did I know that in bulldozing my way to fulfilling that promise, I was about to discover a formula. A formula I repeated three consecutive times, minting two unicorns where alliances were an undeniable part of the journey.

I figured out how to go from nothing, to the #1 partner, to the most important possible partner.

I uncovered an art. How to PartnerUp and win together.

I realized that a startup's goal shouldn't necessarily be to build an ecosystem, but to win inside an existing ecosystem by forming a strategic alliance with the ecosystem parent.

I learned that technology partnerships, service partnerships, and overall partner strategy for an early-stage company should emanate from one strategic alliance at the top, and then surround it.

And now you can too.

What is the purpose of a partner-led executive?

Strategic alliances are not something you need to validate for your Board, CEO, or yourself.

Strategic alliances are for the brave, the bold, the market shifters and category creators. They are for those that play to win.

Strategic alliances result from a fundamental understanding somewhat antithetical to traditional startup advice: not all choices are equal.

Sometimes, you have to call your shot. At that point, you had better damn well be calling the right shot because not only does your job rely on it, the entire company does as well.

The right choice (and execution) can alter the course of your company and possibly even the course of markets toward greatness or colossal failure.

A true partner executive or founder understands that if not all choices are equal, then neither are all partners.

They develop a strategy, call shots, and nail it.

Strategy isn't a dirty word. It's misunderstood.

The best companies in the world often have "partner" or "business development" functions rolled up into some sort of "Chief Strategy Officer" because, to put it simply, **strategy is choice.**

If you are going to play the game of strategic alliances, you have to make better choices than everyone else. Why? Because get in line, everyone wants to partner up with the sumos of your space.

That's what separates a partner executive from just another title. True partner executives know how to make choices no one else can make.

They are entrepreneurs and market makers. They make choices others fail to make. Choice is what separates the professionals from the amateurs.

How do I know?

I've seen the power of winning a strategic alliance as a startup several times.

First at PandaDoc partnering with HubSpot, where we became their number one tech partner globally for CRM and secured HubSpot's first ever venture investment. Then at Drift partnering with Marketo, where we became Marketo's first ever exclusive alliance as a 100-person startup. After Marketo was acquired, we went all in on Adobe, becoming Adobe's first ever exclusive alliance as well and won Adobe Partner of the Year out of 1,700 partners—in our first year of the partnership.

All three of these alliances have one thing in common: within one year, our tiny startups were the most important partnership in a giant's entire ecosystem.

There were term sheets, big deals, legal, travel, hand-to-hand grinding out referrals after building one-on-one trust.

It took everything.

How was all that possible? How were we able to land exclusive alliances and win with the likes of HubSpot, Microsoft, Marketo, and Adobe?

We played to win. Second place was last place.

It's hard. Stupid hard. But for the brave, here's how you can do the same.

The Five PartnerUp Principles

1. Build-In-Market > Go-To-Market
2. Understand Strategic Alliances
3. The Playing to Win Framework

4. Find Your Black Swan
5. Negotiate and Win the Big BD Deals

1. Build-In-Market > Go-To-Market

The market always wins.

Companies? Rarely.

It's amazing how myopic our world can become in a venture-backed startup, looking at the world through the lens of some spreadsheet that spits out results we think we control.

That's Go-To-Market—designing the spreadsheet inside your walls to get the results you math'd into existence.

In today's world, understanding an operating model and unit economics isn't an advantage. It's table stakes. GTM is B2B SaaS entrepreneurship level 101 and that's it.

So, what's the next level?

It's being market-led and building-in-market, instead of merely going-to-market.

Let's take an example: Slack and HipChat.

HipChat had a very similar product to Slack, or at least not different enough to justify a switch. So why did Slack win?

Slack had a much better GTM strategy. They pioneered the freemium product-led growth framework that layered sales on top of product usage and data, and created a far more efficient revenue engine.

And they beat HipChat. But they lost the war.

No one can say that a 27.5 billion dollar exit makes a loser with a straight face.

But the fact is, Slack (acquired by Salesforce) had just over 15 million daily active users and then, almost out of nowhere, Microsoft Teams had north of 125 million!

If they had such a good product and a great GTM strategy, how was Teams able to catch up and lock Slack out of market dominance?

In the walls of the best B2B venture firms, there's a little saying:

"Great product never beats great Go-To-Market."

To be fair, they got it half right.

The reality is actually more like this:

Great product never beats great Go-To-Market, but great GTM never beats great Ecosystem.
Does Microsoft Teams have a better chat product than Slack? I sure don't think so. But they made it MANDATORY, which drove their entire Office productivity suite through their field teams and their GIANT partner programs. They leapfrogged Slack because they drove Teams to all of their channel and tech partners through existing nodes of trust, with the obvious bonus of Microsoft already a line item in virtually every enterprise.

Slack's innovative product-led revenue engine never saw Microsoft coming. Then they got scared, real scared. So scared that Slack took out a full page ad in The New York Times entitled "Dear Microsoft."

It was clever, but to the Microsoft network, it was merely cute.

That's the power of an ecosystem.

No ad, email, or phone call could compete with being directly walked in, no matter how targeted, automated, or personalized.

Again, **the market always wins.**

Build In Market, don't merely go to it.

Build In Market > Go To Market.

BIM > GTM.

So, how do you start?

2. Understand Strategic Alliances

I believe startups are victims of endless opportunity, and first-time partner professionals are perhaps the only ones duped more often than first-time founders.

I've seen it time and time again. They chase after every partner opportunity they see—an inbound big agency; another tech integration; co-selling with a consultant; partner marketing with an industry friendly; and so on.

At a startup, everyone feels like everything they're working on is priority numero uno. But if everything is "high priority" then nothing is a priority.

What's the solution for startups?

You can't build an ecosystem until you win inside another ecosystem.

The PartnerUp method forces choice and says before you build any other partner function inside of your org, you have to become NUMBER ONE with the most important market leader in your category.

You need to land a Strategic Alliance that should drive your entire partnership strategy until you have the network effects and orchestration support to become your own ecosystem.

The problem is the root word in strategic alliances is STRATEGY. And strategy is the most misunderstood word in all of startup land.

Strategy equals choice.

And not all choices are equal.

So, how do you make the right choice and influence the choices that your company makes?

3. The Playing to Win Framework

It was my first day at Drift. I was reporting to the Founder & CTO, Elias Torres.

Elias is one in a million, perhaps one in a billion.

Have you ever met a CTO who didn't have a laptop at the office? That's Elias.

"I build teams, products follow," he used to say.

My first day started with a barrage of WhatsApp messages basically saying I had until Friday and my first Executive Leadership Team meeting to figure out where we place our partner bets.

But something told me this was more than just another meeting. I had a feeling I was expected to be right!

Thankfully, Elias had shown me Playing To Win: How Strategy Really Works.

In very brief summary, Playing To Win has three distinct parts.

1. Strategic Choice Making
2. Reverse Engineering
3. Strategic Testing

The first part, Strategic Choice Making, details five steps of cascading choices to not just call your shot, but to call the right shot.

- What is the winning aspiration?
- Where will you play?
- How will you win?
- What capabilities must be in place?
- What management systems are required?

I worked 24/7 to turn the entire book into a template in my first week:

It's not just about what you say yes to. It's also about what you say no to. As a forcing function, it's a dang challenging exercise.

I highly recommend doing this with your most trusted partner before doing this with your leadership team as an exercise.

(If you are interested in getting a copy of the template slides, shoot me a DM on LinkedIn. Happy to get a copy over to you and help.)

Breaking it down a tad more:

What is our winning aspiration?

- Don't think about money. Everyone is playing for money in business. Start with people. What does it mean to win with your customers and partners?
- What is the competitive nature? Who are you winning over?

Where will we play?

- Market, Segment, Vertical, Horizontal, Geo, Size.

  (Don't make the mistake of choosing your current field of play for ease. It can be, but this is not a descriptive exercise; it's a prescriptive one.) What people are you playing with?

- Channels or Methods. What field are you playing in?

How will we win in chosen markets?

- Simply put, how to win on the field.

What capabilities must we have?

- The activities you must excel at. The more reinforcing the capabilities are of other capabilities, the better the advantage.

What management systems do we need?

- Guardrails, rules, processes, and measures that demonstrate how well the strategy is working.

These five questions are the bedrock for the Playing To Win strategy. They're not a crystal ball, and getting them right certainly takes more than a ten-minute reading (more like ten sessions), but let's put it this way: Can you afford not to have these questions answered before choosing which ecosystem you are going to win in?

The right choice can shift markets. The wrong choice can tank your company.

Be bold, but be thorough. Measure twice, cut once.

Frame your strategic choices to generate possibilities.

Start with a **strategic problem.** You should have multiple strategic problems to work through—and remember, this is about the market, not about you or revenue.

What are the **choices to focus on** to solve that strategic problem?

Reverse engineer your strategies.

You're not done yet.

Reverse engineering ensures your strategic plan has tactical legs and implications across four vectors:

Industry

- Segments
- Structure

Customer Value

- What's in it for them?

Relative Position

- Capabilities
- Costs

Competitors

- Reaction - what will they do?

For each step, you have to be able to say, "It would have to be true that…"

You're not done until you get rid of the "nice-to-haves."

Focus your highest level of intellectual capacity there as a leadership team—this can be where you bring in the rest of leadership.

Ask questions about the market, and don't discuss going to market. The market doesn't care about the problems of your GTM strategy. The market rewards creative solutions to problems it knows it has.

The central node to your PartnerUp strategy, your Sumo, the giant of your space, also doesn't care about your internal problems or processes or choices.

They only care about why you are the most important partner to them.

And their people? They need to believe the same thing for themselves.

The Playing to Win templates are a critical part of the startup alliances playbook. Now that your choice is nailed and you know where you want to win, you need another force on your side.

The "aha!" moment.

4. Find Your Black Swan

When I went to Drift, I took what I had learned from securing the Hub-Spot alliance and built another strategy. The result of the Playing to Win strategy I created at Drift was simple: win Marketo.

If you've followed PartnerUp or PartnerHacker, you've heard from my friend, Jill Rowley, who basically invented social selling… She's a big deal!

In early 2018, when I was setting out to strike this sumo alliance, I was a fan of hers.

Little did I know that she and I would soon meet on the playing field to win, as partners.

In 2018, Jill was Marketo's Chief Growth Officer. She wasn't directly responsible for partnerships, but she was the chief evangelist, and I knew she understood how critical partnerships were to Marketo's future.

I met Jill and two other Marketo executives in San Francisco with my vision for a much bigger deal than just another integration.

We had to WIN Marketo. Be number one. The best. Far above and beyond any other partner. That was the goal.

I had one shot to turn Jill from connection to champion.

We were playing to win, which meant this meeting mattered. I had to nail it.

Turning Belief into Proof

Before even stepping into the meeting, I believed we were going to be Marketo's number one partner, but I needed more than just belief to convince Jill and the partner execs.

I needed proof.

It's hard to prove something before it happens, but luckily, I had read Chris Voss's book, Never Split the Difference. Voss explains that the most important part of a negotiation is, "Finding the black swan."

He describes a black swan as a "Game changing piece of information that neither party knows when entering a negotiation."

So, what was that game changing piece of information? I had no idea, but I knew I had to find it.

Come to find out, finding the black swan isn't a linear path.

The nature of the black swan is completely contextual, which means every company has something different to bring to its target sumo.

Black swans also aren't always obvious, but there is a trick for finding your company's black swan.

Instead of searching for the answer first, make sure you know the right questions to ask.

If you can't answer the right questions, **you will never win the alliance or become critical to their ecosystem.** You just won't.

To unearth the black swan for a B2B alliance, you have to answer two questions.

Question 1 – Company:

"What is the most important metric that is a top three priority for the entire business?"

This could be things like net retention, pipeline growth, churn, activation, conversion, win rates, competitive win rates, and on and on. There are countless permutations and combinations that matter to different companies at different times, all the way up to the Board and CEO.

Make sure your company impacts a metric that the CEO and her team would immediately respond to with, "Yes, that is a top three priority as a business."

Question 2 – Role:

"Which department (and role specifically) is directly responsible for the metric, and which role's **compensation** is directly tied to the metric?"

Tying these two questions together is where the magic happens.

They are the formula for playing to win in alliances because they're how you turn belief into proof.

Back in San Francisco, I was sitting down with the Marketo execs and my friend Bobby Napiltonia, who agreed to shadow the meeting (total power move on my part).

At the table, I set the stage for the meeting, stating, "By the end of this meeting, if we can agree on the answers to two questions, we are going to be high-fiving across the table."

Hours later, the meeting ended with high fives initiated by none other than Jill Rowley.

We uncovered the black swan and turned belief into proof.

Here's what we had learned:

Answer to Question 1

At the time, Marketo's most important metric was Net Dollar Retention. We needed to show that they could effectively grow the subscription price per customer while reducing churn.

Answer to Question 2

Marketo's CSMs were compensated based on Net Dollar Retention. 100% of their commissions were based on customers they owned spending more at renewal than the previous year.

This seems like basic stuff, but here's where the black swan appears through the fog.

What was the most important driver for Marketo increasing the subscription price year over year? **The number of contacts in their customer's Marketo database.**

There are dozens of pricing/upsell levers, but the number of contacts in their customers' databases was the most important to the CSMs and to Marketo. It showed their customers were growing and Marketo was, too.

Keep following here because it hasn't even gotten good yet.

At the time, Drift's basic integration with Marketo took marketing automation concepts used for personalizing email to websites through chatbots.

These chatbots were designed for marketing and sales. They would engage, understand, recommend personalized next best actions for website visitors, and capture new contacts more effectively than the forms on the website, thereby sending more contacts to Marketo.

Boom.

Did you see it? The elusive black swan, IRL.

- By recommending and installing Drift and connecting it to Marketo, customers were capturing more contacts from their website.
- Marketo drove serious results for Net Dollar Retention.
- CSMs were delighted because they could recommend a trusted partner who helped them get paid, delighted their customers, and were impacting the most important goal for their employer.

By answering those questions and understanding how our company and product affected their customers, their company, and their CSMs who were directly responsible for and impacted by contacts in the database, we were able to flip belief into proof.

At that meeting, it was agreed that we were Marketo's most critical partner.

I could go on with another dozen stories about how we took over Adobe Summit and the main stage keynote after that meeting, how we became Adobe's Partner of the Year out of 1,700 other partners, or about how we won over 1,000 accounts from this thesis.

The proof is real.

It's the same formula I used for PandaDoc with HubSpot.

When HubSpot CRM launched, it was in the most competitive SaaS industry: SMB CRM. PandaDoc was an e-sign and proposal tool. At the time, Hubspot was already a juggernaut public Martech SaaS company, but it was so early that HubSpot CRM didn't even have APIs.

I knew they'd win CRM, and we HAD to be number one.

Here's that same formula applied to the PandaDoc and HubSpot alliance:

The year we went after HubSpot, we found out that HubSpot CRM's most important metric was activating trial signups. We also uncovered that the most important metric for taking a signup to a paying customer was moving a deal to Closed Won. Moving a deal to Closed Won meant a 7000% increase in the likelihood a customer paid HubSpot!

And that's exactly what PandaDoc did. It helped people close deals.

We covered the full story on episode 1 of the PartnerUp Podcast, but the short of it is:

- PandaDoc hacked a chrome extension which allowed it to send documents from HubSpot even without access to their APIs.
- We got a few dozen joint customers to use it and even sent a few customers to HubSpot to try it out.
- We discovered that PandaDoc cleared the friction for closing a deal and moving their first opportunity to Closed Won at a faster rate and with higher predictability **than any other single partner HubSpot had.**
- Less than one year later, PandaDoc was HubSpot's number one CRM integration. We were so successful that we even convinced HubSpot to cut their first ever venture check. That's right, this formula won so well that HubSpot Ventures was formed, and PandaDoc was the first ever check HubSpot cut to invest in another SaaS company.

This is the PartnerUp formula.

I've used this formula to establish strategic alliances with three sumos and to advise dozens of other startups.

This formula is only for those bold enough to uncover the secrets and only for those brave enough to Play to Win.

You have the formula; now it's time to close the deal.

5. The Deal is Yours, Not Theirs – Winning the Big BD Deal

This is the final table.

Ninety-five percent of people never get here, and you made it. But access does not equal power.

The reality is, this is the hardest part, and it's only for the wisest and bravest.

Now that you have the knowledge, the validation, the black swan, and it seems like it all feels right, you have to follow it through to the finish line.

Remember this: these are your terms; you are in charge. Not your partner.

This stage is not collaborative.

Whatever you do, don't make this about your alliance partner's template, their standard partner program, or their contract review process.

Sure, you may be a part of their program, which gets you access to APIs or maybe even listed, but that's perfunctory, not a victory. Victory is an alliance deal, a custom contract with real commitments and skin in the game—millions, tens of millions, hundreds of millions, or even billions on the line.

To close these types of company-changing, market-shifting deals, you need to realize **that you are the entrepreneur.**

Ask the sumo of your space to spend insanely costly hours to craft a deal that makes you famous, and money is never going to happen. That's not partnerships—it's you being lazy and entitled to the success you think you've earned up until this point.

Don't lose the race at the finish line. You aren't done.

The entrepreneur who wins doesn't wait for the market to set the terms for them; they create something entirely new based on an unshakable vision. This is your vision. This is not your partner's vision. If it was, they would have already won, and you wouldn't be at the table.

You are creating something new, an asset of value, and you are **bringing** that value and creativity to the table.

Bernie Brenner, the author of The Sumo Advantage, describes Business Development (BD) saying,

"BD is about taking the assets or capabilities of two or more companies and combining them to create a third, even more valuable asset."

So what is that asset? What is the new state of an even more valuable asset?

That's your proposal—the deck, the pitch, just like an investor pitch. Ninety-nine percent suck.

And how does the rubber meet the road?

That's your term sheet—the requirements, the numbers, the commitments. Your terms.

The ones that make everyone a winner, but YOU are the only one that completes the formula.

Control is everything at this stage.

There's very little out in the wild about how to win strategic partnership deals at the finish line. Not just negotiation tactics, but real-life steps that take you from the partner knowing who you are, to not only being important to them, but actually minting the deal.

That high five with Jill Rowley? Amazing. But was it a contract? Nope.

We ain't done yet.

Luckily, as I called out above, there is one little book that's quite the gem to traverse this stage: The Sumo Advantage. It's not perfectly suited to B2B, but the contract negotiation principles are remarkably similar given the nature of those partner contracts being B2B contracts.

According to Brenner, the primary problem BD people face in winning these types of rare but incredible deals is the illusion that you are in control.

Just because you have a seat at the table doesn't mean you are going to win. In fact, by the very nature of you being at this stage, you are already at a disadvantage.

The reality is, because you are the one driving next steps, you force your alliance partner into reactive mode.

They have to react to each move you make, which is both a blessing and a curse. When others are reacting to you, you can't predict their next move. At any point, no matter how far along you are in the process, you're still vulnerable to their "not right now."

The solution: confusion.

Wait, what? No, I'm not talking about dishonesty. I'm saying "don't show up and throw up."

You need to strategically withhold information and create a sense of FOMO. The fear of missing out is driven not by complete information, but by the right information at the right time.

Momentum in these deals can create the illusion that you are ready for the final step of the deal—the contract—but before you go there, take a step back.

At each step, you are doing something important: keeping contracting as the final and perfunctory step. Once legal and procurement and finance is involved, you have lost 100% control.

The goal of the final step of the process is to take as long as you need while pushing forward each step to get the answers to the test.

Getting the Answers to the Test

If contracting isn't the last real test, then what is? The term sheet.

Like meeting agendas, or cadence, the term sheet is never something you should cede control of. Never.

Why?

Because it's all interconnected. The purpose of every meeting and every step is to find your answer to the overarching test.

You have your private term sheet which outlines your ideal state, but it's not the answer to the test.

The term sheet is the necessary list of bullets and basics of the deal which would change the game for you and, you think, your partner. It also outlines your private set of "walk away conditions," where the deal doesn't make sense any longer.

You get the answer to the test by working backward from the term sheet.

The question you need to answer is: How will you reach the goal at the end of the alliance rainbow and ensure that by the time you present the first term sheet to your sumo, you've already won?

That answer will allow you to drive the agenda.

In the immortal words of Sun Tzu, "Victorious warriors win first and then go to war."

Done correctly, once you've answered that question, you've already won the war.

There's a reason why so few strategic partnerships exist.

Most lose before they ever go to war.

Most take the test, only to find out they got the answers wrong.

If you have the opportunity to help your growing business land an alliance, to win in an ecosystem before you try to build your own from scratch, good luck.

If you pull it off, you'll be a market maker.

You'll earn the respect of leaders in an industry, not just your company.

You'll change your company forever.

And you'll change your life.

PartnerUp and Play to Win.

I'll see you in the arena.

Account-Based Networking 101

By Adam Michalski

Adam Michalski is the CEO of Partnered, newly acquired by Cross-beam. Partnered is the network where B2B sales teams share customer introductions.

This article was originally published on the Partnered website.

What is Account-Based Networking?

To crush it in sales, you need to find the perfect balance between finding qualified opportunities, personalizing your outreach, and building trust in the sales cycle. But it isn't easy.

Here's the problem:

- 57 percent of salespeople miss their quotas due to lack of qualified opportunities.
- 74 percent of salespeople struggle with personalization.
- And leading salespeople say trust is the single hardest thing to build in today's increasingly digital sales ecosystem.

Yikes! So... how do you find tons of new qualified opportunities, personalize your outreach to ensure you land a meeting, and instantly gain meaningful client trust?

What if you could tap into a magic network of people that your prospects already trust and they could introduce you and your solutions in a unique, differentiated, and personalized way? It turns out, 90 percent of B2B buyers instantly trust referrals from people they know.

What if this magic network was reciprocal, in that they would introduce you to their customers that are your prospects and you could do vice versa? After all, 77 percent of companies that utilize co-selling see a direct increase in sales.

What if this new way of selling became your go-to-market super power? Sixty-three percent of businesses leverage co-selling to reduce the amount of time their salespeople have to spend in the never-ending prospecting grind.

This magic network is your Account-Based Network, and it's taking off as the future of sales.

The best part? You probably already have a massive account-based network.

Whether you know it or not, your company has already aligned with other tech partners and agencies who can provide you and your sales team with these referrals (along with recommendations, information on who to sell to and when, and more).

These tech partners and agencies are part of your company's "partnership ecosystem" and the smartest sellers in the world know this is the most impactful network a seller has (with 5X more signal than LinkedIn!).

Want to know the science of tapping into your account-based network to close more deals?

Here is everything you need to know about account-based networking, why it's important, and how to use your existing account-based network to close more deals today.

What is Account-Based Networking (ABN)?

Account-Based Networking (ABN) is the modern sales strategy of connecting with other salespeople to share prospect introductions, recommendations, and information to mutually close more deals, together.

You can think of your account-based network as the combination of three sales networks:

1.   Your Personal Sales Network

If this isn't your first sales job, you have likely built relationships with other salespeople throughout your career. Some of these salespeople will have already worked with your prospects—but this account-based network is likely small.

2.   Your Team's Sales Network

If you're working in sales at any B2B SaaS company, you likely already use LinkedIn to connect with other salespeople on your team to help with introductions and information on prospects they have already sold. This account-based network might be bigger than your personal network, but it's still not enough to change the game.

3.   Your Company's Sales Network

This is where it gets interesting. If you're working in sales at any B2B SaaS company, your company has likely already begun investing in their partner ecosystem—i.e., tech integrations with complementary, non-competing products and relationships with agencies that have massive influence over your prospects. This is where your account-based network grows explosively because each one of those partner companies has a sales team that now has a reason to work with you (and this network is often 100X the size of your personal network and your team's network—combined!).

So what if you could easily and directly connect sales teams across your company's sales network to instantly use each other's contacts, influence, and relationships?

Put otherwise, what if you didn't need to start every deal from square one?

You might be thinking that you've already tried this (i.e., what has historically been called "co-selling"). The catch is that up until recently, building these account-based networks was incredibly manual—requiring exporting data to find overlapping accounts across sales teams, getting that data in front of your sales team, getting them to actually take action on it, and then ensuring that these relationships would grow into meaningful (and attributable) partner sourced and influenced revenue.

But account-based networking is different from co-selling. "Co-selling" is a term derived from days pre-dating SaaS where channel partners would go-to-market together, often selling their individual solutions as one cointegrated solution.

Account-based networking is different because the entire ABN framework is built around modern day B2B SaaS sales teams.

Account-based networking allows you to leverage your partner ecosystem to find out who influences your buyers.

This allows you to ensure that both parties get mutual go-to-market value predictably and at scale.

It's also a proven strategy—the best B2B SaaS sales teams are already crushing their quotas by deploying ABN.

What's even cooler is modern tools like Partnered can get you started with ABN in less than five minutes.

Imagine being able to speak with someone who already closed the deal you want to close.

Ice-cold calls become nuclear-hot introductions. Opportunities become easier to create, quicker to close, and sales cycles decrease for everyone in your new social sales circle. Wins get spread around like cake at a party.

Remember the adage sharing is caring? In this case, sharing means hitting quotas.

But, it isn't all about grabbing quick, easy sales and moving on to the next person.

You want to create high-value partnerships with other awesome sales teams.

In an account-based network, you're building long-term relationships with other salespeople which will reap dividends for your entire sales career. Here's the great thing: in ABN, everyone is bringing something to the table. Every new client you land also gives fuel to your partner. And every great new relationship your partner builds helps you fill your prospecting pipeline to overflowing.

So... how exactly do sales team networks work?

Sales Team Networks: Unlocking Your Account-Based Network

Today's buyer's journey is complicated. The average SaaS company doesn't get to run through three simple, step-by-step phases and churn out a lifelong customer with a mind-blowing LTV. In SaaS, you have to get the deal and then resell your service to that client every single month. You can't afford to just do things the way they've been done; you have to do everything you can to understand the prospect holistically so you can ensure your deals have the greatest probability of success.

We sat down with Jay McBain—Principal Analyst of Channels, Partnerships, and Ecosystems at Forrester—on the Partnered Podcast and discussed some of the complexities involved in modern SaaS co-selling. As he pointed out, B2B businesses can find immense opportunities in sales team networks. By overlaying your company's tech and agency partners' customer journeys with your own, you can create better overall experiences for everyone involved.

In fact, there are nearly limitless opportunities to drive partner sourced and influenced revenue across tech and agency partnerships in the B2B SaaS space, especially with cross-selling and upselling baked into the customer journey.

"In the SaaS business model, you have to earn the customer, you have to upsell the customer, you have to cross-sell the customer. And because of that, there's just an inherently different way to partner and utilize partners in that sales cycle to drive additional business value"

—Jay McBain | Principal Analyst of channels, Partnerships, and eco-systems at Forrester

Sales team networks are a **shared relationship between at least two sales teams that aren't competing in the exact same market space.** In the past, these partnerships mostly existed between friends or just among your internal sales team. Today, with ecosystems exploding and companies investing more than ever in building out these relationships with complimentary companies, you can't afford not to connect sales teams for account-based networking. Or if you do, your sales organization is going to quickly get left behind by competitors who take advantage of this tectonic go-to-market shift.

Best of all, you can use tools like <u>Partnered</u> to easily deploy account-based networking best practices with little effort, and you can get started for free. Creating your sales team network no longer has to be time-consuming and difficult for sales reps.

What if you could learn information on your prospects like:

- Who to sell to
- When to sell them
- How to sell them
- and more…?

And here's the kicker: the sales team that shared this data with you isn't losing anything. In fact, they're gaining

something: a relationship with you.

The more sales partners you work with, the bigger your network grows. The bigger your network, the **<u>more sales</u>** you and your partners get.

It's like LinkedIn, but better. Everyone wins.

Why is Account-Based Networking Important?

Whether you are the Head of Sales or just starting your sales career, your account-based network can make or break you. When it comes to account-based networking, the larger your sales network is, the more likely you are to consistently find qualified leads and hit your quota.

Qualifying leads and prospecting are the two most challenging parts of a salesperson's job.

Most B2B SaaS sales teams don't know the potential they are sitting on in their account-based networks. And even if they do, today, only about five percent of sellers are effectively utilizing their sales network. (Funny enough, these are usually the top performers—they've figured that ABN is the cheat sheet to consistently crushing quotas.)

As Andy Whyte, author of MEDDICC - The Ultimate Guide to Staying One Step Ahead in the Complex Sale, pointed out on the Partnered podcast, "We've been trained our entire lives to know that your network is your net worth. And yet the biggest network out there, your partner ecosystem, is oftentimes not utilized."

What happens when the 5% of your sellers that are effective at utilizing their sales network turns to 95% of your sellers?

Every seller can be a top salesperson if they're given the right network access and tools to effectively use ABN.

Welcome to the future of sales.

Winning With Smart Account-Based Networking

Are you tired of grinding just to miss your quota? Why should your sales team navigate every prospect from square one? Join the revolution and make your entire sales team up to 50% more effective by building impactful partnerships with other hard-working sales teams.

Rather than just pushing your product, your sales team members will become trusted advisors by getting an expanded view of the prospects' needs and understanding exactly who to sell to, when to sell to them, and how to sell them. In return, you and your partners both get more sales, create more opportunities, and grow stronger businesses. The more partners you work with, the bigger your account-based network grows.

Who Uses Account-Based Networking?

Most salespeople can agree on one thing: prospecting is hard. In fact, over 40 percent of salespeople believe it's the single hardest part of their job.

To win new clients, you need the perfect combination of opportunities, trust, and personalization.

Case in point:

- 72 percent of companies with less than 50 new opportunities each month don't hit their bottom-line revenue goals.
- 80 percent of B2B buyers expect personalized interactions.
- 88 percent of B2B buyers will only purchase from a salesperson they trust.

To win in today's hyper-competitive sales arena, you need a massive social network to help you find and secure high-value leads. And today, building those social networks is easier than ever.

Who Can Use Account-Based Networking?

Well... you can. Seriously. Every salesperson at every type of B2B company will find tangible value in account-based networking.

Co-selling isn't just for Account Executives anymore. Account-based networks can help at every stage of the sales cycle.

Let's break it down.

B2B Sales Development Representatives (SDRs)

As an SDR, you need to do everything in your power to break into new accounts.

You're dealing with buyer fatigue, saturated channels, and more.

It's getting harder to land those meetings even for the best of the best.

Let's get out of those saturated channels for a minute. You have a massive account-based network of people who are already interested in working with you. Ask them for the info you need to turn that "no thank you" into a "let's book a meeting."

Great partners can help you figure out the best time to approach prospects based on their experience with them. They can also give you insights into how to break into your target accounts. However, for partnerships to be successful, you have to stay in sync with your partners by sharing the right data and insights with them as well.

Stop the churn and burn. Be 100x more strategic and use your network to find the people who can open the door for you.

Looking for more insights? Check out our SDR Playbook.

Account Executives

Let's say your SDR passes along a qualified prospect—amazing. Now it's your job to turn them from prospect to customer.

The first step: you have to hop on the phone with that prospect. By leveraging your account-based network, you can now go into that meeting with all the information that matters.

Use your account-based network to build a "cheat sheet" for how to navigate that deal and build relationships with everyone your prospect already trusts.

It only takes a couple of conversations with contacts they've worked with to ease their skepticism and validate your company.

Long story short: Close deals 40% faster and for 233% more money using account-based networking (ABN).

Customer Success Managers

As a Customer Success Manager, your job is to ensure the customer is successful and that business is renewed or increased, if possible.

Staying connected with your company's account-based network will help set you up for success. Building and maintaining partner relationships will make your life easier in the long run.

The average enterprise has around 130 SaaS applications. This means that your solution is just one piece of their puzzle. To ensure your customer is successful with your solution, you need to think about the big picture. Look at how your technology works with their entire tech stack. This is how you can become a trusted advisor and guarantee your renewals and upsells.

Tapping into your account-based network allows you to connect with all the stakeholders in your customers' sphere of influence, get a better picture of your customers, and be more strategic.

Sales Directors

As a Sales Director, you're the coach supporting your Account Executive team to score the highest number of points. You have a number your team needs to reach, and by tapping into account-based networking, you can hit that number and then some.

The partner team is the best way to close those deals and break into new accounts.

Bold statement, but it's true.

On a tactical note, every 1:1, you should look at the partner ecosystem (or use Partnered) to hold your AEs accountable. If they're not tapping into their account-based network, they aren't doing their job. Period.

Using an account-based networking tool like Partnered gives you the insight into your team's network to help you be the coach they need to get to the next level and hit those goals.

Partner Managers

As a Partner Manager, your connection to account-based networks is the most straightforward.

Rather than having to be the human glue that ties sales teams together, you can be much more strategic.

How? Well, it's not a human problem. Tech is the only way to connect all these dots at scale.

Effective partner managers use modern ABN tools (like Partnered), which allows them to be much more strategic when looking for ways to grow their partner ecosystem.

Stop playing telephone and let technology amplify your abilities so you can maximize your partnership potential. Let technology do the busy work—you focus on building more strategic partnerships that will actually move the needle.

Revenue Executives

Whether you're the VP of Sales or the Chief Revenue Officer, as a revenue executive, you own the entire "number" and need to figure out how your business will hit that number.

Some of that pipeline you can attribute to marketing and some you can attribute to sales. Historically, it's been a struggle attributing pipeline to partnership efforts. That's changing.

Account-based networking is the framework that allows revenue executives to not only insert best practices into the entire sales org for working with partners, but also for tracking each interaction so you can quantifiably report on how these interactions are increasing your pipeline.

ABN is the future of sales because ecosystems are the future of business. McKinsey predicts that by 2025, ecosystems will represent 30% of the global economy, up from 1% - 2% today.

As a revenue leader, you need to adapt to this coming networked world or get left behind.

Winning with Modern Account-Based Networking

Are you tired of grinding just to miss your quota? Why should your sales team sit in the dark alone? Join the revolution.

Expand your account-based network by building impactful partnerships with other hard-working sales teams.

By sharing relationships with your partners, you both get more sales, create more opportunities, and grow stronger businesses together. The more partners you work with, the bigger your account-based network grows.

GoToEcosystem – How B2B SaaS Embraces the Ecosystem

By Allan Adler

Allan Adler is a world-class Ecosystems coach, consultant and change agent. He is the creator of the GoToEcosystem Framework and guides XaaS CEOs and C-Suites to unlock the potential of Ecosystem Orchestration. He's currently the CEO and Managing Partner at Digital Bridge Partners.

Excitement over Partner and Community Ecosystems is at an all-time high—there is even a rumor that CEOs at SaaS companies are fully bought in and Partner Professionals have all the resources and support they need to crush it.

Unfortunately, the rumor is false, but you knew that after you saw this. What CEOs do acknowledge is that Digital Transformation is and will continue to reshape markets and that new business models will be mediated by and through Ecosystems. What they don't know is how that will happen or the strategies that will allow them to grow and thrive with and through Ecosystems.

The Foundations – GoToMarket is Outdated: We Need a New GTM

Markets (as the organizing paradigm for where and how commerce happens) have been fundamentally altered by digital transformation and business partnerships. Ever since currency replaced barter as the way goods and services are transactionally exchanged, buyers and sellers and/or partners and suppliers have interacted based on linear, stove pipe relationships, from making, to marketing, to selling, to distributing, to consuming goods and services.

Digital transformation has blown up the outdated Markets model by restructuring long-held customer value, relational and customer economic principles. Look no further than your last Uber ride to see this in living color. We now take these mobile-first, digital-first, asset-free, network-effect business models for granted. They have changed everything in B2C and are now in the early innings of transforming B2B markets.

The long-standing GoToMarket Mindset is based on outdated ideas about how to deliver solutions to customers built on a closed-market vs. an open-market mindset. In a closed-market mindset, we build and go to market alone through market stovepipes. In an open-market mindset, we co-innovate and attach ourselves to the ecosystems to create sustainable business flywheels.

Ecosystems Require a New Mindset

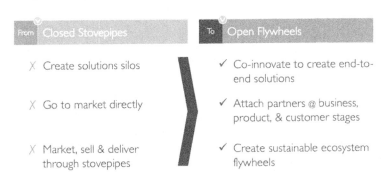

The GoToEcosystem Imperative

Where does this then leave those of us who run or work in the Partner or Ecosystem Orgs within our businesses? The good news is that the very fact that you work in the partner org means that your CEO has actually given you the Keys to build and drive your Ecosystem. The bad news is that He/She has also given Keys to other functional organizations like Product, Marketing, Sales, and CS and that they are better able to marshal resources, leaving most partner people with limited budget, and thereby limited impact. These functional orgs have a hard ROI ($1 investment = X$ return), whereas most Partner teams do not have this hard ROI return model in the bag.

To help solve for the problem of lack of resources and low partner investment prioritization, in concert with PartnerHacker, Digital Bridge Partners has created V1 of the GoToEcosystem Maturity Model to help Partner Leaders achieve three objectives:

1. Systematically evaluate the current maturity of partner and community strategies, processes, and results.

2. Develop a game plan that leverages best practices to overcome challenges and address gaps.

3. Drive impactful transformation to turn Ecosystems into a top three imperative for the CEO and Board.

The GoToEcosystem Framework

In early 2022, Digital Bridge Partners landed the GoToEcosystem Model, a three-part transformation framework based around Strategy, Alignment, and Orchestration. GoToEcosystem is now widely viewed as the first comprehensive approach to unlocking the vast potential of Partner and Community Ecosystem and is targeted initially at B2B SaaS Companies. Here's a picture of the framework for those who are not familiar with our posts.

3 Steps

- Build an Ecosystem Strategy

- Align your Organization

- Orchestrate your Ecosystem

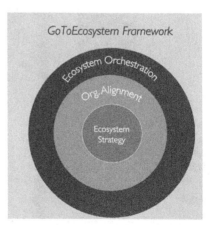

The GoToEcosystem Maturity Model

The GoToEcosystem (G2E) Maturity Model, designed around the Ecosystem imperatives of B2B SaaS companies, articulates a Four Stage Ecosystem Journey that aligns to the Strategy, Alignment, and Orchestration in the G2E Framework. Here are the Stages and associated focus areas, objectives, and key results:

Launch
- Define and establish Ecosystem Strategy
- Select Beachhead Segment Tech Partrners
- Create priority integrations

Prove
- Define aligned cross functional ecosystem processes
- Establish value propositions and messaging and engage Co-Marketing & Co-Selling
- Launch ecosystem program

Scale
- Expand partner segments and coverage
- Lead with ecosystem solutions
- Standardize cross-functional ecosystem processes and build out new "Eco Tech Stack"

Embed
- Ecosystem a Top 3 CEO priority led by Ecosystem Chief
- Ecosystem KPIs shared across organization & network effects
- Establish Eco Ops team and integrate Eco & Functional Org Tech Stacks

Becoming an Ecosystem Business

We are often asked about the outcomes companies and their CEOs can achieve in transforming to become an "ecosystem business" and what the key dependencies are for success.

Our GoToEcosystem Opportunity Matrix summarizes the two key dependencies: aligning partner programs across the organization to increase partner value and moving from a product to a network business model:

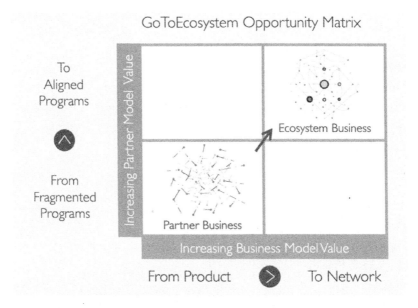

Aligned Programs

Program Alignment happens when all the groups in an organization, including Product, Marketing, Sales, and

Customer Success, both understand and leverage the power of partners and where:

- Partners and Communities are embedded across the organization.
- Partner ecosystem results are reported "through" (not outside) each organization.
- Partner offerings are aligned and integrated with product roadmaps and solutions.

Network Business Model

Transformation to a Network Business Model occurs when market network effects kick in based on platform-driven, third-party co-innovation, and where:

- Partners are attached to > 90% of deals.
- Partners and communities build > 25% of the Product IP.
- Business model is powered by Network Effects.

Outcomes

GoToEcosystem performers like Salesforce, HubSpot, Atlassian, ServiceNow, and Twilio provide a great example of the outcomes ecosystem businesses achieve, including growth, profitability, and valuation:

These organizations serve as Ecosystem Business Superstars that other companies can aspire to follow.

Getting Buy-in From Your Leadership

As noted in the GoToEcosystem Maturity Model above, a company doesn't become a true Ecosystem Business until the Ecosystem is an inherent element of the business, supported across all functional organizations, as illustrated in Stage 4 of the diagram above. In this stage, the partner ecosystem becomes the blood that flows through the organization, rather than being a disposable appendage. This is also when partner attach is supported across the business, in product and customer life cycles rather than only being a source of tactical revenue.

Luckily, many of the well-known B2B platform players—e.g., Microsoft, Salesforce, Atlassian, Hubspot, etc.—provide plenty of examples which point the way to becoming an Ecosystem Business. Be prepared to talk about these examples. If you need some pointers on how these companies managed their own ecosystem transformations, check out my friend Avanish Sahai's outstanding podcast series, The Platform Journey.

To be credible with your CEO and company leadership, Partner Leaders need to present a two- to three-year plan which walks your CEO through the stages of the Maturity Model, explicitly articulating the following critical steps:

1. **Start:** Clearly identify your current stage so everyone understands exactly where your company is on its Ecosystem journey.

2. **Crawl:** Your short-term plan (< 6 months) to complete the current Maturity Model stage as measured by specific business outcomes, with leading and lagging indicators.

3. **Walk:** Your medium-term plan (~6-12 months) which will prepare you to take on the challenges of the next stage of the Maturity Model.

4. **Run:** Your long-term plan (~1-3 years) that describes how you will get to Stage 4 and achieve full Ecosystem Business maturity.

Driving Cross-Functional Transformation

Delivering ecosystem results is predicated on gaining cross-functional buy-in for your ecosystem strategy and plan and transforming your organization, from your CEO, to product, marketing, sales, customer success, and beyond.

Requirements for Transformation

Organizational transformation depends on three change model levers and principles—Commitment, Focus, and Delivery. And it's worth noting that it often falls on Partnership Leaders to drive the change management agenda across each of these levers, including:

1. **Commitment:** Gaining the commitment of cross-organizational leadership to the fact that partner ecosystems can enhance both company-wide and specific organizational outcomes.
2. **Focus:** Focusing on achievable change levers, initiatives, and outcomes aligned to shared OKRs across the organization, aligning the partner and other orgs.
3. **Delivery:** Being relentless and delivering tangible outcomes in order to institutionalize and sustain cultural change.

The Alignment and Transformation Journey

The journey begins with alignment across the organization. As noted below, five key constituents—your CEO, Product, Marketing, Sales, and Customer Success teams—must come together to operationalize a Go-ToEcosystem Strategy:

An important foundation of success is acknowledging that change won't happen all at once. Transformation requires a journey. Organizations must build trust and create momentum with initial quick wins aligned to a realistic maturity model. The Digital Bridge Partners Go-ToEcosystem Maturity Model discussed above sets forth four stages of evolution: Launch, Prove, Scale, and Embed.

Outcomes at each stage of this journey build on each other and align to specific groups within the company, to drive the organization towards maturity. Examples include:

- **Launch:** Here, two critical organizations must be engaged: the Product Team to drive key integrations with beachhead partners and the Customer Success Team to validate and document integration success.

  Prove: At the Prove stage, the focus shifts to demonstrating ROI. Marketing drives co-marketing campaigns and Sales drives co-selling plays for specific use cases validated in the launch stage. It is essential at this point to demonstrate quick wins and an initial business case to all involved, including the C-Suite, and gain buy-in.

- **Scale:** At this stage, the focus shifts to a greater emphasis on top-down alignment, planning, and engagement across the organization. Standardizing cross-functional processes and shared OKRs becomes essential, including automated account mapping to scale results with and through Partners.

- **Embed:** With Embed, the organization evolves from a focus on individual 1:1 team alignment and engagement, to many-to-many alignment and engagement. OKRs can now move from a focus on planning within individual organizations to company-wide planning with KPIs across the CEO & C-Suite. At this stage, Ecosystem Ops are essential, including integrating ecosystem Tech Stacks across departments, including functions such as automated account mapping, sales, and marketing ops.

Call to Action – Plot an Achievable Course

Driving organizational change throughout the maturity model and journey, and delivering ecosystem outcomes, is dependent upon best practice change model levers and principles:

1. Listen, Empathize, and Gain **Commitment:**

    *   Openly commit to a simple, compelling, and shared organization-wide vision founded on experience, understanding, and trust.
    *   Build a grassroots, diverse, inclusive movement enabled by executive leadership and mandates.
    *   Create a guiding coalition that includes both internal and cross-organization and external stakeholders.

2. **Focus** and Empower to Achieve Immediate Results:

    *   Focus on executing achievable change levers, initiatives, and outcomes.
    *   Empower and collaborate by removing hierarchy and barriers to execution.
    *   Demonstrate commitment, build trust, and create momentum with quick wins.

3. Be Relentless and **Deliver** Tangible Outcomes:

    *   Maintain executive roadmap accountability, involvement, and sponsorship.
    *   Institutionalize and sustain commitment and inter-organization cultural change.
    *   Focus on achieving realistic, tangible, initiative-based outcomes and align to aspirational KPIs.

Don't be shy about asking for help from Partner Pros like Digital Bridge Partners who have done this before. The GoToEcosystem community is a generous group of folks. Guidance, best practices, and coaching are a Slack post or a DM away.

From Partner Enablement to Ecosystem Enablement

By Jessie Shipman

Jessie Shipman is CEO of PartnerFluent, just in time partner enablement that combines event planning and account mapping.

Fifty percent of Sales time is wasted on unproductive prospecting.

Sales used to be the first step in a customer's journey, but it's not anymore, and most sales teams haven't fully adapted.

For Sales teams to adapt properly, Sales Enablement must champion the transformation by setting a new precedent and facilitating an internal shift.

Instead of remaining sales-facing, organizations will need to become Ecosystem/Platform-facing.

The organizations that see this shift coming and adapt to it will find themselves ahead of the organizations that do not. For that reason, Sales Enablement teams are approaching a critical moment and need the right information to take advantage of it.

Since 2017, Sales Enablement adoption has grown 343%. There's no surprise as to why. Sales enablement programs have had an incredible impact on revenue organizations.

Seventy-six percent of organizations see an increase in sales between 6-20% when they have a sales enablement program.

Sixty-percent of best-in-class organizations have formal competency in sales enablement.

Teams with a sales enablement strategy are 52% more likely to have a sales process that is tightly aligned with the buyer's journey.

Eighty-four percent of sales reps hit their quotas when their employer incorporates a best-in-class sales enablement strategy.

What is sales enablement?

Forrester defines Sales Enablement as,

"A strategic ongoing process that equips client facing employees with the ability to systematically have a valuable conversation with the right set of customer stakeholders at each stage of the problem solving lifecycle to optimize the ROI of the selling system."

You can find many different Sales Enablement definitions, but core to all is that sales enablement ensures effective customer conversations by providing sales teams with the right content and knowledge.

Hallmarks of traditional sales enablement programs are centered on content. Connecting people to content, presenting content, providing content for pitching, and measuring the effectiveness of the content.

Sales enablement tools, then, provide a single source of truth for all customer-facing content and how to use it. When sales enablement programs are at their best, they attempt to close the alignment gap between sales and marketing.

In the decade of the ecosystem, it has become apparent that the alignment gap between sales and marketing can really never be closed, even by the best enablement.

Instead, the greatest economic returns will be seen by the organizations that embrace the mindset of platform + ecosystem and begin adopting the structures and strategies that align.

When you embrace ecosystems, with all of their nuance, required agility, and orchestration, you have to revamp ideas around what customer-facing roles should know and do, and how ecosystem enablement professionals help them get there.

Transforming Sales Enablement to Ecosystem Enablement

In order to understand how to transform sales enablement to ecosystem enablement, it's important to underscore the principles of the ecosystem.

Historically, the core question at the center of channels, alliances, partnerships, etc. has been, "What are you going to do for me?"

That question is fundamentally flawed.

The good news is that this perspective is shifting and partner professionals across industries are starting to ask, "What can I do for you?" as the first step in approaching new partnerships.

This me-to-you shift in mindset impacts six foundational elements of the ecosystem:

Co-Innovation

Co-innovation is step one in developing an orchestrated ecosystem. How do organizations find ways to co-innovate? How do they find ways to fill in the gaps in each other's offerings? How do they work together to solve for recognized needs in the customer buying cycle?

Sphere of Influence

Once an organization has decided on its solution and determined how it will fit into partner ecosystems, it turns to leverage the ecosystem's influence. Influence is the new marketing. In order to help customers discover new solutions, ecosystem participants want to share their spheres of influence with their partners.

Co-Selling

Traditionally, sellers were responsible for one solution—theirs. Ecosystem selling, instead, is collaborative. Initial conversations are focused on establishing trust and understanding needs. Then, partners are brought into conversations as value-adds to the ongoing relationship

Value Realization

Integrated products are better together. Revenue teams that leverage their ecosystems see larger deal sizes, shorter sales cycles, higher close rates, and higher retention rates.

Network Effects

Highly effective ecosystems use relationship-based network effects to drive monetization, expand customer bases, and become stickier.

Trust and Sustainability

Ecosystems exist to be of service. They create and leverage trust to provide a win/win/win between themselves, partners, and customers. The nature of this trust spurs additional innovation and the ecosystem flywheel spins faster and faster.

The Portal Problem

In the same way that sales enablement relies on a single source of truth, partner enablement has, historically, been centered on activities and assets that require an individual to seek out learning through some kind of content management or partner portal.

The "what are you doing for me" mindset causes most partner enablement efforts to be outward-facing, which results in a multitude of disparate portals with scattered information.

Only 17% of marketing budgets are spent on partner-facing materials, and 90% of B2B sellers don't use enablement materials because they're irrelevant, outdated, and difficult to find and customize. Seventy-two percent of IT service partners aren't able to connect partner offerings to buyer needs and challenges, and 65% claim that the quality of partner content is either poor or impossible to find. Forty-two percent of sales reps say they don't have enough information before engaging a customer.

This old way won't work in the new ecosystem model where top sellers must learn how to combine and design individualized solutions using platform and ecosystem.

By 2025, $60 trillion of global revenue will flow through ecosystems. Ecosystem Platform business models, a model in which partners and communities create network effects by co-innovating around a platform or platform features, will require a new kind of sales mindset. Sales cultures and sales enablement must change to help sellers embrace this new mindset.

Eighty-five percent of sales leaders believe that sales teams will need to be skilled at customer problem analysis and solution selling. They'll need to learn how to do networked account planning, and communication and relationship-building will become critical skills. However, only 55% of those leaders believe that their teams are currently equipped to make this transition.

Ecosystem Training and Enablement

Ecosystem training should aim to create the critical skills that are necessary for effective selling in the coming ecosystem economy.

Skills cannot be taught with a video, a quiz, or a one-pager. Ecosystem skills enablement will require a blended learning approach.

Blended learning looks at learning outcomes first, and then identifies which training objectives can be matched to the outcome.

Blended learning incorporates knowledge transfer with skill practice, application of new behaviors, performance assessment, and just-in-time performance support. Learning involves not just remembering information, but manipulating, combining, and innovating with the information.

Sellers will need to be provided opportunities to role play, to experiment, to observe these new skills, and then the safety to try them with their customers while being provided coaching and feedback. KPIs will need to be built around these skills, and sellers will need to be monitored and measured on their application of them.

Building an ecosystem enablement program around blended learning recognizes that encoding, or moving information from short-term memory to long-term memory, should be done as much as possible, and in the same environments or scenarios in which sellers will need to retrieve the information. This is called in-context learning.

Most corporate training and seller training gives little attention to the needs of learners. In prioritizing scale, this compliance mindset has eroded the development of high-quality learning content.

Adult learners are primarily self-directed. They bring their own experiences to the table. They are motivated by change and are eager to learn the things that help them to solve problems and improve their lives.

As an org attempts to build a blended learning approach to ecosystem enablement, keep in mind the *Knowles Four Principles of Adult Learning:*

1. **Adults learn best when they are involved in the planning of their learning and development**

Find ways to involve your sellers, or a cohort of your sellers in the planning of their learning. Conduct a needs assessment and ask them (in a way that gets you unbiased answers) what they are currently doing (around the skill), what they wish they understood, what they wish they were, and perhaps how they prefer learning.

It's not helpful to record and store a video series in a Content Management System if what your people really want is a Slack group where they can collaborate to share stories and wins and ask questions.

2. **Adults learn best when they are able to act on and reflect on the skill they're trying to improve.**

Providing actionable, reasonable KPIs that sellers can strive towards is the most impactful way to engage them with a change in behavior. Ensuring that these KPIs meaningfully impact a seller's day-to-day performance is critical to not frustrate the seller. Reflecting on these KPIs frequently with a coach or mentor will help the seller to embrace the new skill through accountability.

3. **Adults learn best when they are challenged by problems, rather than merely hearing solutions.**

In truth, we don't really have many solutions to offer. Everything about changing seller behavior from product selling to ecosystem selling is a new frontier. The best thing to do is to create an agile ecosystem enablement program that takes into account seller feedback, highlights seller innovations, and changes as quickly as environments change. Organizing in this way will allow the sellers to take ownership of problems, innovate new solutions, and create learning pathways.

4.   **Adults learn when a subject is relevant or is something they care about.**

Motivation is tricky. For Sellers to find the information relevant, executive leadership must clearly delineate between Ecosystem and revenue generation.

An ecosystem feeds and surrounds a sales funnel, so learning how to sell in an ecosystem directly impacts the seller's livelihood. Executive buy-in, company culture, and agile enablement should all help to overcome a lack of motivation.

Enablement Evolved

Enablement will have to become so much more than a repository of content. It will have to become cross-functional.

It will have to become Ecosystem Enablement.

In the past, the "what can my partners do for me" mindset kept everything separate. Partner enablement was separate from both sales enablement and other partner enablement teams.

The ecosystem mindset aims to consolidate partner enablement into a single source of truth, alongside and in collaboration with sales enablement. This consolidation of partner learning assets is critical to the success of ecosystem enablement and is positive proof for partners that an organization is committed to elevating their joint value proposition. An organization that commits to enabling their sellers through ecosystem offerings and positioning has clearly embraced ecosystem as a primary revenue driver.

Ecosystem enablement will take a number of successful functions of sales enablement, embrace what works, and evolve what no longer does.

Sales enablement worked well because sellers were only required to understand and position their product. Sales enablement provided a foundation of understanding and was able to scaffold additional information on top of existing motions.

Sales enablement could function as a repository for specific content because positioning products isn't necessarily dynamic, but Ecosystem enablement cannot function like that.

Ecosystem offerings are, by their very nature, complex and evergreen. Because of this, ecosystem enablement will need to be dynamic in its delivery. It cannot only provide access to a static playbook, or battle card, or one-pager.

Robust ecosystems will have multiple players that may provide a solution to a complex customer problem. No solution will be one-size-fits-all, and every customer will likely benefit from a different set of partners. Not only that, but the joint value proposition of one partner to another will potentially change when you add in additional partners, making for a multi-tenant value proposition.

Static content in a repository will not be enough to enable sellers in this scenario. Because of this dynamism, it's not fair or feasible to ask an individual seller to be well-versed on every partner in an ecosystem.

Building Robust Ecosystem Enablement

To create the best Ecosystem Enablement, we must pull from many different learning theories and best practices.

The first best-practice is consistency. Consistency is useful because it prevents decision-fatigue. Current partner enablement materials can be wide-ranging in their consistency, making it difficult for the seller to find what they need, and then able to articulate it to the customer.

Another best-practice is storytelling. Stories are a critical component to memory, particularly when we connect and create our own stories around a subject. Leveraging a simple, consistent framework for partner enablement information allows the seller to learn quickly what they need to know.

Given these best practices, the first step in building Ecosystem Enablement is consolidating individual partner information into four key areas:

1.   What the product or platform is

A seller or CSM doesn't need to know the in depth workings of a partner's product or platform. They need to know at a basic level what it is, what it's supposed to do, and who should use it.

2.   What is the Joint Value Proposition

This is the kicker. Sellers need to know how the products make each other better because of their partnership. This needs to be in its simplest terms. JVP addresses which gaps in their own product the partner fills and then helps them articulate it.

3. Co-Selling Questions

This is a list of questions the seller could use in a customer conversation to determine if this solution is a good fit for a customers problem. It's something they can use while on a customer call.

4. Partner Enthusiasm

Partner enthusiasm will help the seller to understand how committed the partner is to building and following through on solutions with them. In here should be links to case studies, colleague feedback, and any incentives that the seller may receive from the partner.

But even with a simple framework, expecting a seller to memorize these four parts for each of the partners in your ecosystem is unrealistic. Instead, this information needs to be accessible performance support.

Seller Enablement

The next question you may be asking yourself is, "How will sellers know when they need it?" This is where an Ecosystem enablement system goes from a product, to a platform.

Ecosystem enablement platforms will need to leverage AI or event-based learning triggers to help sellers get the right partner information at the right time, preferably just before they engage a customer. Ecosystem enablement platforms will need to think first about seller tech stack integrations so that partner learnings will be a part of their everyday workflows, and help them to engage their ecosystems through the ever-widening ecosystem tech stack.

In this new paradigm of Ecosystem Enablement, the seller's new motion would be something like this:

- The seller sets up a meeting with a customer through networked account planning and is now in the ecosystem mindset. This seller wants to be curious, ask the right questions, and help craft a solution for the customer using their ecosystem.

- Thirty minutes before the customer meeting, the Ecosystem Enablement platform notifies the seller that their upcoming meeting has a few partners that may be a good fit, based on previous interactions and account mapping.

- The seller clicks or taps on the notification and it brings them into the learning platform where they quickly review the four parts of the partner learning framework to prepare themselves for the upcoming meeting. Armed with the co-selling questions, they enter into the meeting with curiosity and ecosystem top of mind.

- During this meeting, the sellers will use problem analysis skills to craft a solution. They ask co-selling questions from the ecosystem enablement platform and determine that one or more partners may be a good fit. They present the joint (or multi-tenant) value proposition to the customer and propose a follow-up call with their partner. The customer agrees.

- At the end of the call, the seller uses the ecosystem enablement platform to reach out to an AE at their partner company through account-based networking and hops in the partner portal to register a deal. Finally, they use the integration with a partner engagement platform to send relevant materials as a follow-up to the customer and to set up the co-sale meeting.

Ecosystems are the Future

Imagine the kind of impact this workflow could have on revenue, ecosystem, innovation, and reciprocity. Deployed at scale, businesses could become more connected, driving more mutual benefit and more innovation. Complex customer problems will be solved through innovation and collaboration, rather than brute force, or half-baked execution.

Ecosystems are the future of business, and Ecosystem Enablement will be a critical pillar to the success of that future.

Thank You To Our Launch Partners and Contributors

Without you, none of this would have been possible. You are helping to define this new decade of the ecosystem.

Printed in Great Britain
by Amazon

14820958R00088